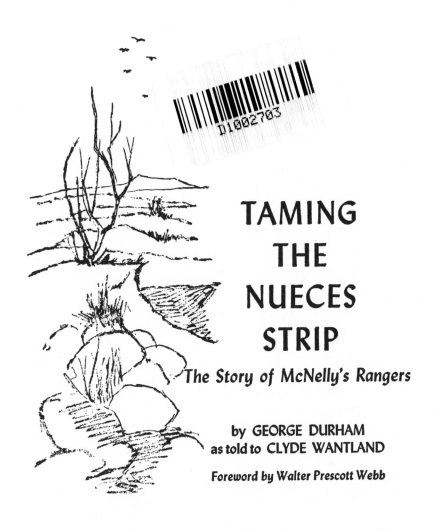

TAMING
THE
NUECES
STRIP

The Story of McNelly's Rangers

by GEORGE DURHAM
as told to CLYDE WANTLAND

Foreword by Walter Prescott Webb

UNIVERSITY OF TEXAS PRESS, AUSTIN

Requests for permission to reproduce material from this
work should be sent to:

     Permissions
     University of Texas Press
     P.O. Box 7819
     Austin, TX 78713-7819
     www.utexas.edu/utpress/about/bpermission.html

♾ The paper used in this book meets the minimum require-
ments of ANSI/NISO Z39.48-1992 (R1997) (Permanence
of Paper).

ISBN 978-0-292-78048-4
Library of Congress Catalog Card Number 62-9795

TAMING
THE
NUECES
STRIP

The Story of McNelly's Rangers

TO

PATRICK IRELAND NIXON, M.D.

A friend of humanity

A lover of Texana

FOREWORD

This singular little book, *Taming the Nueces Strip,* is a true adventure story with so many unusual features that it is sure to be prized by collectors of Texana. In it George Durham tells of his experience as a Texas Ranger serving under Captain L. H. McNelly for a period of about two years, 1875 and 1876. George Durham did not write the story, but told it to Clyde Wantland, a trained reporter and writer, and Wantland put it down as Durham told it more than fifty years after the event. One feature of the story is its simplicity. It is about George Durham, the youngest man in the Ranger Force, and his captain, L. H. McNelly, and what they did in restoring some semblance of law and order to that part of Texas lying between the Nueces and the Rio Grande, the Nueces Strip. Of course, other characters appear, but their role is not important. Durham is concerned with what he did, what he saw, what he thought in following the Captain, the leader whom he worshipped, with good reason.

The time of the action recorded is brief, less than two years, and the years themselves are important, 1875 and 1876. The acts of McNelly, and his "little McNellys," as his followers proudly called themselves, can be better appreciated, understood, and justified when we see them against the backdrop of the general conditions existing in the state during these two critical and tumultuous years. Without some knowledge of this background the reader might have difficulty in understanding how a peace officer could be as ruthless as McNelly was.

It was in the period between 1874 and 1880 that the Texas Rangers did their greatest work. They had then their finest opportunity, because the state was full of things requiring their attention. The Comanche Indians were still raiding in the western half of the state. The interior was plagued with lawless men, often organized into mobs, engaged in feuds which terrorized whole counties, such as the Sutton-Taylor feud in DeWitt County and the Horrell-Higgins feud in Lampasas. Horse thieves and train and stage robbers were numerous and elusive.

The Nueces Strip stood out as something special in the way of brigandage, murder, and theft. It had more than its share of domestic criminals led by King Fisher and his friends, and it had besides an international band of cow thieves under the leadership of Juan N. Cortinas, who had been operating from Mexico since 1859.

This was the condition after the Civil War, when Texas was going through the ordeal of reconstruction. The government, imposed by a combination of military rule and political disfranchisement, was breaking down, and the best element in the state was doing all in its power to contribute to the debacle, which came in 1874 when Richard Coke was elected governor in place of E. J. Davis, the carpetbagger. Governor Coke took immediate steps to restore some semblance of order in Texas. Under his leadership the Legislature created the Frontier Battalion of Texas Rangers, which went west to drive the Indians back, and then turned its attention to the outlaws of the interior. This famous band was under the command of Major John B. Jones.

The Nueces Strip, being an exceptional case, was given separate treatment. A Special Force of about thirty men was organized and placed under the command of Captain L. H. McNelly. No better man, probably, could have been found for this assignment. He was a frail man, then dying of tuberculosis, but he managed to live a little more than two years, and to make a record unmatched among Texas Rangers of all time. He was a natural partisan fighter if there ever was one. He entered the Confederate service at about the age of seventeen and was soon operating mainly within the Union lines. Equipped with an iron will and totally unacquainted with fear, he acquired the art of taking care of his minority in the presence of a majority. It is a tribute to him that he was given any command in Texas at all, because he had served for a short time in the hated State Police during reconstruction.

George Durham, a green kid from Georgia, joined McNelly at Burton and followed him to the end of McNelly's career. Durham then entered the employ of the King Ranch, which lies in the Nueces Strip, and remained there until his death. It is often stated that the historian cannot depend on accounts, such as Durham's, given long after the event. This is generally true, but I think there are exceptions and I think two of the exceptions can be found among McNelly's men: George Durham is one and William or Bill Callicott is another. When I was writing the history of the Texas Rangers I found McNelly's official reports to the Adjutant General of the events narrated by Durham.

Also I had the recollections of Bill Callicott, and now we have George Durham's story. A comparison of their accounts with McNelly's reports indicate that the memoirs of both men are remarkably accurate. There is no doubt that the experiences these young men had with their intrepid leader were the most dramatic and exciting events they ever knew. They had something to remember, something to live over and over, and to talk about with their comrades. The story burned itself into their brains so that they remembered it when they had forgotten many later but far less exciting incidents. McNelly is, of course, better on dates, but his little McNellys are better on side events and episodes. Bill Callicott had the gift of making himself the center, if not the hero, of many episodes; George Durham was more self-effacing. Both men had one thing in common, and they must have had this in common with all their companions, the worship of the frail man who knew how to take them into danger and bring them out alive. They justified everything he did, including the unvarying execution of prisoners thought to be from a foreign country.

It was McNelly's misfortune that he was not at the Alamo or Goliad, or at some other place where his courage, ingenuity, and audacity could have been exercised in a patriotic cause. Had he performed the remarkable feats there on behalf of freedom that he performed in the Nueces Strip, mainly on behalf of a few stolen King cattle, he would have been a heroic figure in Texas history, but he would not have been any greater than he was in the eyes of the young men who have done all they could to perpetuate his memory.

WALTER PRESCOTT WEBB

CONTENTS

ILLUSTRATIONS

INTRODUCTION

I asked the postmaster at Raymondville if he knew George Durham. The graying old fellow eyed me with evident astonishment.

"I reckon," he replied, "that you're a new man in these parts."

I nodded slow agreement. "I came down to try and meet Mr. Durham."

"That," said the postmaster, "needn't take much trouble." He glanced at his calendar. "This is Wednesday, ain't it? Mr. George comes in for his mail on Wednesday. He'll be along shortly."

Just to make conversation I remarked, "Now, this is the George Durham that worked for Captain McNelly?"

"Yes," the old fellow replied simply. "Mr. George is a McNelly. I reckon he's about the only one left. That all happened quite a spell back."

"When Mr. Durham comes will you point him out for me?"

The little post office was busy. A steady stream of people

came and went. The streets were what the Chamber of Commerce would call bustling. Farmers from far and wide were starting life anew in this fabled land of deep soil and mellow sunshine. Their wagons and farm trucks stirred a ceaseless cloud of dust.

"That won't be necessary, son," the postmaster told me with a trace of tolerance. "When the biggest man in the biggest hat shows up and folks nudge each other and point to him—that's George Durham."

And that proved to be the precise sequence.

I first saw George Durham as he squirmed his huge frame from behind the steering wheel of a Model A carry-all. He emerged a leg and a shoulder at a time. When he was all out in the clear he tapped the pockets of his brush jacket; shook his pants back into normal walking position; removed his huge hat and reshaped its high crown; surveyed the Model A with casual tolerance; and started across the dusty street.

The postmaster was right. No one need tell anybody that here approached something solid in a human shape. First, he had the external appearance of a working man. Nothing phony, nothing dressy, nothing gaudy. Just a working man. Could be the foreman of a cow camp.

He walked directly toward his target—the post office. He looked neither right nor left. Moving with the majesty of the Katy Flyer backing into a station, he found a path cleared for him. The enraptured crowd just naturally fell away.

I accosted him boldly as he stepped up on the board sidewalk.

"You're Mr. Durham—that right?"

"That's right," he replied, without missing a step.

"I'm a writer—"

He halted and glanced down at my mere six foot. "What sort of a writer?" he inquired.

"I work for a magazine. To get a story on Captain McNelly and a picture they—"

"You all aiming to print a story on Captain?"

"Yes, sir."

"Well, get it straight before you print it."

"That," I assured him, "is what we want to do. That's why they sent me down to try and see you, Mr. Durham. You did work for Captain McNelly, didn't you?"

He turned and faced me squarely, as if the question had been totally unnecessary and something of an insult. Then he nodded slowly, reflectively.

"That's right. I'm a McNelly. My father was a McNelly in the war. I've been a McNelly all my life. I expect to die a McNelly. And when I get Over Yonder, I want to go back to work for the Captain if he's still running an outfit."

"I wonder if you have a picture of Captain?"

"Yes, Caroline—that was my wife—got hold of one a long time ago. It's in her trunk, out at the ranch."

"Reckon you'd let—"

"When I get my mail," he replied, somewhat throatily, "I'll buy a cup of coffee and we can talk it over."

He—George Durham—had just offered to buy me a cup of coffee. That meant something, a mighty big something, to a free-lance writer. It meant that I had broken down the barrier that had shielded writers and storytellers from George Durham for more than half a century.

The simple facts of history proved that George Durham must now be crowding eighty; and the archives at Austin indicated that he was the sole surviving source of the full story of the fabled McNelly group of Texas Rangers. The Captain himself had neither the time nor the inclination to write a blow-by-blow account of his historic cleanup of the Nueces Strip. Only a Ranger who had been there could do that, and George was the only one still alive.

There was nothing dramatic about that nickel cup of restaurant coffee. Nothing historically significant. The course of no empire was changed that day. But to me it lingers as a cherished memory. It launched an acquaintance that, for my part, matured into friendship. It began an association with a man whose image time has only enlivened.

We dawdled over the coffee for probably half an hour. And for once I yielded to my instincts and kept my mouth shut. I only answered questions about myself—and measured my words carefully, realizing I was under the scrutiny of a master scrutinizer.

I passed the test successfully.

"If you want to," he said, pushing back his chair and rising, "you can follow me out to the ranch, and I'll show you that picture of Captain."

I followed along a dirt road leading east for ten or so miles, and we stopped before an unmarked gate. It was a huge gate with a fifteen-foot span, built of rough, unpainted two-by-eights. It was crude, but most certainly substantial.

George took a key from his pocket, unlocked the gate, and swung it open. We entered. He stopped, got out of his car again, and returned to close the gate. I followed.

He looped the heavy chain into place, snapped shut the lock, gave it a testing tug, and said, "I'll show you where to get the key." He walked behind a mesquite and placed the key in a crotch. "When I'm here," he explained, "the key'll be there. When I'm not here, the key won't be there." I got his meaning.

I had a feeling—a feeling since validated—that inside the big gate was a world all its own—a world that pretty well lived its own life, made its own rules, minded its own business, and demanded the outside world do the same.

I followed George Durham about half a mile down a dirt trail and we approached a frame house. Like the gate, it was big and substantial, and unpainted. He motioned me to a chair on the gallery. "Have a seat," he invited, and he went inside. The chair was crude and aged, but substantial. The hair on the hide bottom was worn off except around the fringes. The legs were steadied with twisted baling wire.

George emerged carrying a battered shoe box that he deposited on a round table. Then he sat down in a rocking chair. For the first time, he now removed his hat and laid it beside the shoe box. He surveyed me again and presently explained—without apology, just reminiscently—"This place has sort of run down since Caroline went on to be with the Lord. That was in 'fifteen. Captain King built us this house when we were married in 'eighty-two. Caroline was a niece of Mrs. King.

"We came here right off when we were married. Never lived in any other house. We raised ten children here.

"This is El Sauz division of Captain King's ranch. He made me foreman when we came down. I'm still foreman. This old house is still in pretty good shape. The ranch has talked of fixing it up, but I talked them out of it. I promised Caroline that nobody else would ever live here but us, and I hope they tear the old house down when I go on to be with Caroline and Captain.

"When you write that story about Captain McNelly I might help you out with some things I jotted down through the years as they came to mind.

"This is Captain's picture. I'll let you borrow it if you'll pledge to give it back."

I naturally made the most of Durham's invitation to call on him for help. But I moved cautiously, to avoid pressing my luck too far.

I waylaid him in Raymondville the next Wednesday and we went through the coffee routine with hardly a variation. Anxious to get another invitation to follow him out to the ranch, I brought up the subject of Palo Alto.

"I wonder, Mr. Durham," I led off, "if you'd go with me some of these days and help me make a sketch of that battleground."

"No. No siree. I won't. Some fellers from Texas University wanted the same thing. But it's against Captain's orders. One of his rules was never to go back over the ground of a scrap. But I can give you the list of Rangers in that scrap. Captain led sixteen of us in. I've heard of at least a hundred who say they were in it. But there were sixteen— I'll give you their names if you want to follow me out to the ranch."

Our Wednesday meetings soon became a fixed habit.

Hoping for, and anticipating, many more to come, I rented an apartment in Harlingen, brought my family down from San Antonio, and enrolled the children in the Harlingen school.

Presently I began carrying to our Wednesday meetings a typed draft of my previous notes, which I left with George for his perusal until our next meeting. In this leisurely tempo the McNelly story took shape and the incidents were placed chronologically. Evidently convinced I was trying to get the material correct, Mr. Durham mellowed and talked freely, checking incidents from yellowed papers in the big trunk and reliving some of the stirring incidents with enthusiasm.

Between Wednesdays I browsed through the Valley for material on some other free-lance stories and assignments. Every time George Durham's name was mentioned I got a new image of him. He had become more than an institution; he was a legend, especially in law-enforcement circles.

At that time he had been a resident of Texas for nearly sixty years. He had been under just two bosses and had drawn pay checks from only two sources: Captain McNelly and Captain Richard King—and King's successors. He had been a peace officer the entire time—either a Texas Ranger or a deputy sheriff. Veteran officers estimated that Durham had "handled" more than nine hundred outlaws and wanted men. Durham told me this figure was "about right, counting the raiders from across the river."

In George Durham's book there were only two kinds of people—the outlaws and the law-abiding. There were no big or little, no brown or black, no white or red. His respect for the orders of his superiors and his regard for the majesty of organized law were part of the legend. His only known abiding hatred was for the gaudy, swashbuckling "bad man."

"Those fellers with their gun butts all notched," he told me, "are the easiest arrests an officer can make. They've killed many; yes. Killed soda jerks and limber drunks. It's always a pleasure to take one out of circulation."

George Durham—like his idol, Captain McNelly—was a deeply religious man. Like his idol, his unbelievable courage stemmed from a belief that the time of a man's going was fixed the day he was born into this world and that nothing he could do would change it. He would die at the proper time, before the blazing muzzle of a gun, or under a roof between clean sheets. Only the Good Lord knew those things.

As a practical stockman Durham was reckoned as a top hand. His judgment as to the combined heft and value of any given herd was uncanny. He had always a clear picture of the grazing potential of every one of the two hundred sections of El Sauz.

He lived one day at a time, making quick and inflexible decisions as problems and challenges arose. "I never carry over any of today's worries," he told me. "That way I get a good night's sleep and make a new start at daybreak the next morning."

As I took my final leave of George his parting admonition was: "The way you've put down that story is fairly good and the facts are straight. Captain wasn't a hero, and don't you let those fellers change things to make one out of him. He only did his duty as a peace officer—and he wouldn't want you to make it look any different.

On May 17, 1940, George Durham died in the house built for him and Caroline. He was eighty-four.

This is his story, pretty much as he told it. Some grammatical corrections have been made in the interest of readability. But none of the facts he gave me have been tampered with. This is Durham's own account, as accurate as his memory and those yellowed papers in the big trunk could make it.

CLYDE WANTLAND

TAMING
THE
NUECES
STRIP

The Story of McNelly's Rangers

The Nueces Strip

Ranger Recruit

Around my farm home down in Georgia, Captain McNelly was a bigger war hero than General Lee. My dad served under Captain McNelly with his Texas guerillas in Louisiana. He said that General Lee made his plans first and then fought; that Captain McNelly made his plans like a chicken hawk—after he had located his target and was coming in for the kill.

Dad outlasted the actual war; but he didn't outlast Sherman.

For several years I did the best I could to help out and get the farm back to making a living for the family. But we had to start with no stock, no tools, no chickens—nothing much but a house that had been plundered.

Lots of our neighbors in the same fix pulled up stakes and went to Texas. The way we heard it, this was a fairyland where beeves by the thousands ran loose and belonged to anybody with a rope and a branding iron and able to hold his own.

I pulled out for Texas in the spring of 'seventy-five. I was nothing but a big hunk of a farm boy straddling a plow horse, with a few victuals and a pistol.

Right away after I crossed into Texas I began asking about Captain McNelly. Was he still alive? Where could he be found? In mighty near every settlement someone knew the Captain, either direct or by reputation.

I drifted up along the coast, inquiring here and there, and wound up in Washington County, where folks told me Captain was farming a headright of cotton over near Burton.

The Burton post office was in the back of the little drugstore and soda fountain. I asked the postmaster if he knew Captain McNelly.

"Sure, I know him," he said. "You a friend of his?"

I told him my story. I only wanted to see the Captain and maybe shake his hand.

The postmaster then told me, sort of confidential: "McNelly will more than likely be through here today. I sent a letter to him last night by messenger—I thought I'd best rush it to him as it was from the Governor's office. It might be important. It's a safe bet the Captain will go through here to Austin to look into it."

There was a girl waiting on the soda fountain, and two or three of the local boys were squandering their nickels on soda water. I strolled up and did the same thing. My nickels were mighty scarce; but I figured I'd never find a better spot to spend one or two. She was a mighty pert little trick and I was sipping my soda and getting some talk under way when a little runt of a feller entered, nodded to everyone, and ordered a dollar's worth of black cigars.

As he left, the postmaster hollered to me, "That's him! Better catch him!"

"Naw," I answered. "The Captain McNelly I wanted was the one that led the Texas scouts in Louisiana during the war. The old Captain."

The postmaster shook his head. "That's him. There ain't but one Captain McNelly. There'll never be another. That's him. You can tell your younguns you saw him. If you want to speak to him better get going."

I did. I overhauled him as he climbed into the seat of a light carryall. He was rolling an unlit cigar in his mouth.

"Captain McNelly," I said, "I'm George Durham, from Georgia."

"All right," he said crisplike. "What can I do for you?"

"My dad worked for you in Louisiana."

"Did he get back?"

"Yes, sir, but Sherman got him."

"Uh huh."

He nodded to his Negro driver who clucked and shook the lines. They had a span of rangy, fifteen-hand, well-matched mules, and they took off in one of those smooth, ground-eating paces that made mules the choice of folks who wanted to go the farthest between suns.

I stood and watched the rig trail off to the north in a cloud of dust. And I still stood. This had all happened in less than a minute. But it had done something to me. I had pictured the Captain McNelly I came to see to be a picture-book sort of Texas fighter. Big and hairy, with his pistols gleaming. What I had just seen could have been a preacher. A puny one at that.

I went back to the drugstore, but I didn't yearn for any more soda water or talk with the little lady. I went straight up to the old man.

"How long, you reckon, before the Captain gets back from Austin?"

"From where?"

"From Austin."

"How do you know he's going to Austin?"

"You told me."

"I did not." The old man came up close and gave me some of my first and best advice. "I reckon I told you too much. That letter was Captain's business. I shouldn't have meddled and blabbed about it. From here on if you want to know any of the Captain's business ask the Captain. He won't tell you, but he'll give you a look that'll stop your meddling."

My feathers fell, and I felt sort of droopy. I felt that the little lady behind the soda fountain and all the others in there were snickering at me.

I moseyed out to my horse and took the reins off the hitching rack. I backed off a ways and looked him over. He was a good farm horse, but clubfooted and sway-backed. My saddle was the cheapest sort of a hand-me-down. I climbed aboard and let the old nag have his head. He was pointing east; and we cantered back that way.

For a little while I mulled over the idea of riding on back to Georgia. Boys my age get funny ideas at a time like this. Back home, of course, they would sure snicker at me—I had taken off for Texas with such a show.

Off to the right I saw a big flat field of maybe forty acres. This was planting time, and two teams were breaking and seeding it. I rode out and asked the man if he needed a hand. He looked me and my horse over and said yes.

"I'll pay you fifty cents a day and found," he said. I went

to work—the same kind of work I had left Georgia to keep from doing. I worked six days, collected my three dollars, and went back to Burton.

I had done a lot of thinking and had both my big feet on the ground now. I admitted I wasn't yet a man. But I wasn't licked. I had come to Texas to make my own way and maybe get a start. And now I had three dollars cash that I could jingle.

You know, clinking silver dollars has always done something to me; sort of like having a blooded horse between my knees. I went back into that drugstore and banged down one of the dollars and told the little lady to set me out a soda.

The old man came up and asked, "Where've you been, son?"

I barely noticed him and said, "I think it was you that told me not to go around asking questions."

He drew back and scanned me from head to foot. "Well, well. I'll be dogged. Son, you'll probably make it. You'll make somebody a good hand. Good, sound body. Plenty of size. Captain would probably sign you on. You got a horse and pistol. He'd pay better than chopping or planting cotton. And the work would be steady."

"What Captain?" I asked, coming alive.

"McNelly. He located a camp yesterday, three miles out west on the Corpus road. He's hiring men. He'd maybe take you. Why don't you ride on out and give it a try?"

I gulped the rest of my soda, raked in my change, and did just that.

There were a dozen or so men clustered here and there; and under a spreading oak there was a little tent with a table in front and a man doing some paper work. Captain McNelly was walking around, his hands deep in his pockets, an unlit cigar dangling from his mouth.

I didn't feel a bit bashful or scared. He looked at me and I looked at him. He didn't say howdy. I didn't say howdy. Pretty soon he spoke. "You're that lad from Georgia."

"Yes, sir."

"You want to sign on?"

"Yes, sir."

"Do you know what this is?"

"No, sir."

"This is a Ranger company."

"Yes, sir."

"You still want to sign on?"

"Yes, sir."

"Do you own a horse and saddle?"

"Yes, sir." I pointed.

"Do you own that pistol you're wearing?"

"Yes, sir."

"Can you hit a target at thirty paces?"

"Meaning a man, sir?"

"Certainly."

"I don't know, sir. I never tried."

He half-circled me and sized me up from every angle. I tried not to flicker an eyelash. He went over to the big feller at the table, took his soggy cigar out of his mouth, and said, "What do you think, Sergeant?"

The big feller said slowly, "I think he's worth a chance, Captain. I'd risk it."

Captain turned to me and said, "Your pay will be thirty-three dollars a month in state scrip and found. You furnish the gun; the state will furnish the shells. You want it?"

"Yes, sir."

He turned to the big sergeant and said, "Sign him up."

I broke out a big grin, I reckon. As near as I recollect, this was April 25, 1875. It was the biggest day in my life up to then. And sixty years later, I still reckon it as one of the biggest days—the biggest next to the day Caroline married me.

Here I'd ridden all the way from Georgia to get a job in Texas—had turned around and started back. A day or so ago I was a farm hand. Now I was working for Captain Mc-Nelly as a Texas Ranger, just as my dad had worked for him as a scout.

I felt some chesty. Just a country boy, but I'd caught on fast. As time went on I learned that the most important lesson a man could learn on coming to Texas was to keep his mouth shut and not ask questions. I had learned that and just now passed that test.

Now that I was one of them I thought I'd be friendly and mix with them. They were bunched in twos and threes here and there, and some were alone. For the most part they were emptying their saddlebags, and cleaning and oiling their gear. None of them had more than five pounds of mess gear and all. One or two had an extra shirt. They were traveling light.

As I'd walk up, they'd look at me and say nothing. I sauntered on until I came up to one who was turning gray, sort of, and he smiled and nodded.

He was whetting a knife on a piece of sandstone. I watched and wondered if I ought to have a knife. His wasn't a pocket knife. It had an overall length of a foot or better, a good part of it being a copper-covered handle. It shone like good metal and was sharp on both sides.

I watched him for a spell and then tried to make some talk. I grinned and said, "My name's Durham. George Durham."

He was through, so he got up and replied, "Shore 'nuf?"

Later on, when we served together, I learned he was signed on as Jim Boyd. Still later I learned he was on the dodge from California for killing an army officer, among

others. I also learned, from watching him one moonlight
night, that he was by far the best knife fighter who ever
crossed my path.

Him being an older man and seeming to know his way
around, I cottoned onto him and watched what he did and
how he did it. I was a green hand, and I was trying to learn.

I didn't have any gear to fuss over, so I had nothing to do
but mosey around and try to strike up some talk. I felt
mighty good—felt like I was all of a sudden a man. I had
been hired by Captain McNelly, the same as the rest of
them. I was as big and as good. And I had to talk.

One feller had a pretty fair-sized piece of tarp spread
down and quite a bit of gear, including an extra shirt and a
big box thing that looked like a camera. I learned later he
was signed on as Parrott, and that he was a part-time pic-
ture-taker, drifting through the country.

Being as I had to talk, I said to him, "Wonder where
we're going?"

He got up off his hunkers, stretched himself, looked me
over in a sort of a fatherly way, and said, "Hadn't you
heard?"

"No," I replied.

"This is a sort of a secret," he said, "but we're going where
the Captain says go. Where he takes us."

That set me boiling. I bristled and fired back, "I've had
enough of that damn smart-aleck talk. I asked a question. I
can't make you answer, but I can damn sure make you stop
jawing back at me."

He broke out in a pleased laugh and slapped his thigh.
"You're a good bet, son," he said. "You'll either make it or
else you'll go down trying."

In a minute he said, "I don't know, but I'd say it's a good
bet Captain will take us into Corpus first. They're having a
heap of trouble lately. Those raiders from across the river

hit the Corpus country a while back. Burned down three or
four of the settlements, killed several good folks, and raised
hell in general. I was in Corpus last week and the whole
settlement was forted and expecting the raiders to hit any
time.

"It'd be a good guess that Captain will throw us at that
bunch as a starter."

Moving Out

That guess proved to be right. By sundown we had twenty-two men, who'd ridden in one at a time. The word had got around and they came in from all directions at odd times. I was the youngest of the lot. Most of them gave you the idea they had fought in the war. On which side was their business. Captain didn't ask, of course.

He didn't ask much of anything when they came up to the table. He looked them over, pretty much as he'd done me, and either took them or cut them back—like buying saddle horses.

But those he took had something. They showed the wear and tear of a hard life. Their clothes were heavy and coarse, made for work. Their boots were scuffed and worn. Their faces were stubbled or bearded and usually deep-furrowed. Somehow you wouldn't pick a one of them to push around.

Their pistols were a part of their clothes, same as their boots and hats. They weren't decorations. They were sizing each other up, and weren't friendly or unfriendly.

The wagon master bellowed, and we gathered up our mess gear and filed by. Each got a helping of frijoles and a good hunk of johnnycake. Those that had a cup got coffee. I didn't have a cup.

As dark began gathering, the big sergeant who had been at the table hollered the command to fall in. I didn't know what that meant, but I followed the others into a single line. It was, of course, a military command. I found out then the sergeant's name was John Armstrong. When the line was formed he passed down and made a nose count.

Captain appeared out front and Sergeant Armstrong reported, "There's twenty-two, Captain."

"Does that tally?"

"Yes, sir."

Captain commanded, not too loud, "Count off by eights." The men seemed to understand that order, and did it.

"All number eights, step forward two paces." When they had done this, he continued, "You'll be acting corporals until further orders. You'll be held responsible for the men in your dab. You'll post a guard of four men in three-hour tours, beginning at the head of the line."

He stopped a minute, then said, "It'll be all right to light up some fires. When you bed down—bed down at the ready at ten-pace intervals, behind your mounts."

These were all military orders that I knew nothing about. But most of the men did, and those who didn't had sense enough to do as the others did.

My corporal had signed on as Williams—Polly, he came to be called. He was a man now beginning to gray up some, and he had sure had service somewhere. He knew orders and how to obey them. And he also seemed to know a heap about Captain McNelly.

I was caught in the third watch that night and was sleeping sound when Williams shook my shoulder and roused me. That was one mighty good habit the old-timers didn't have to teach me—to be able to sleep when sleeping time came. When you can do that you don't wear out so fast.

Williams shook my shoulder and I came up right sharp. I had my hat on and my pistol holstered by the time I straightened up full. He watched me in the dim light of a last-quarter moon.

Then he advised me in a fatherly fashion, "Son, it's your turn to stand guard three hours, and standing guard in this outfit means just that. Stand, don't sit. Don't even hunker. We ain't in enemy country yet, so far as we know, but we're on a war footing, under war orders in Captain's books. If you'd be caught napping on guard—well, Captain can't order you shot, but he can bounce you out of this outfit with a black mark that'll go down on the books and follow you to your grave."

Well before daylight action began around the supply wagon. The wagon boss was Dad Smith, and he brought along his son to help. The boy cut the wood and looked after the fire. He was a boy about my age, and we came to know him as Febe.

My corporal waved me in and I fell in line for breakfast—corn mush and one slice of side meat and coffee. This boy Febe got me a cup and poured me some coffee. I had never drunk much coffee, as it was a mighty scarce item back in Georgia. And after sipping some of this I doubted if the coffee habit would ever get much hold on me. But it sure picked you up and started your innards grinding and your brain whizzing. It was home-parched and powerful.

The rest of the hands went back to killing time, and so did I. Captain and Sergeant Armstrong were busy up around the table as men began riding in from here and there. One bunch of four rode in from Burton. Three more came in from the north. Captain was looking them over and Armstrong was doing the book work.

I sauntered over to Boyd, who had that knife out whetting it and shining it up. He looked up and said, "Ever play cards, son?"

I said, "Some."

"Got any favorite game?"

"I've played more stud than anything, I reckon."

"I got a deck," he said. "Want to kill some time?"

I said yes, and he cleaned off his tarp. He laid down some money and I threw out my jingling cash.

I didn't seem to learn too fast. In no time all my money was over in his pile.

"That all you got?" he asked.

I gave a sheepish smile and said it was.

"Well," he said, throwing my coins back, "neither of us is going to be spending any money for some time, and a boy needs some walking-around-money in his jeans. Take it. When we get to where we can spend it I'll win it back off you for keeps."

Dinner time came and went and nobody said anything. For myself, I was a little hungry. But I saw Dad Smith latching up the endgate and loading his cooking gear.

Sergeant Armstrong ordered us back into line, new hands and all. There was quite a line. He counted us off again and turned to the Captain.

"There's forty-one, Captain."

"Does that tally?"

"Yes, sir."

Captain waited a minute then ordered, "As I call your

names, you come over here. L. B. Wright. J. B. Robinson."

They came up to the Captain and faced the line, and Captain said, "These men are your lieutenants."

He called out two more names—R. P. Orrill and L. L. Wright. When they came up he said, "These are sergeants. John Armstrong is your first sergeant."

With the introductions over, Captain said, "Be ready to move out in fifteen minutes."

I had no gear to gather, and I had my nag saddled and boarded and in line behind Polly Williams in plenty of time.

Sergeant Orrill with two Rangers galloped out ahead of the line and fanned out in patrol. We moved out behind them on the road to Corpus Christi well ahead of sundown.

I hadn't eaten since breakfast, and neither had my horse. But I learned that when the outfit was on the move eating could be put off. And we were now on the move. It sure beat killing time around camp.

The way Captain fixed control over this bunch can't be told. I still don't know how he did it, but he did. One thing, he didn't waste a word or a move. He appeared to know exactly what he wanted to do and how to go about doing it. I got the feeling that here was a man who could tell you what to do and you'd do it and never have any suspicion that he might be wrong. In less than two days he had put together a bunch of men of all sorts and made an outfit that moved like old hands. Some of them he knew from years past. That was the reason he made them officers. He had picked them all for only one reason—to him they looked like men who would take orders and fight.

The talk later on was that many of these men were on the dodge and were wanted in other places. A story is still making the rounds that one of them was the old Missouri guerilla, Frank James. For myself, I don't know and don't

give a damn. They were all good enough to be hired by
Captain McNelly. That was then, and still is, good enough
for me.

We moved all night at a brisk walk, and I sometimes had
to jog that old plow horse of mine. He came near to shaking
my kidneys loose. An hour or so before daybreak we saw
water off to our left as we moved in close to the coast. We
skirted the upper end of the bay before sunup and headed
south to Corpus.

Corpus Christi was a fair-sized settlement at that time.
There were one or two big stores and a considerable number of little ones. (In case you wonder how I know names
and dates and details of a lot of things, just remember that
in the fifty-odd years since it all happened lots of us have
talked it over around cow camps a thousand and one times.
Times and things in this country are sort of dated by Captain McNelly—"that was before McNelly," or, "this was
after McNelly." The farther the years moved us away from
the man, the bigger he and his time looked.)

As we rode into Corpus Christi that morning, I wouldn't
have known that it was Corpus unless someone had told
me. I recollect the town seemed mighty quiet for a settlement its size. There were no women or children on the
street. And mighty few men.

The reason was that they were ready for a bandit raid.
They were forted as best they could be—had their window
shutters drawn close and all hands inside, except for a few
outside on errands.

I later learned that at the time McNelly rode into Corpus
with his new Ranger outfit that April morning in 1875 the
river bandits were swarming all over the area, having a big
time. This was the first time they had raided so far across
the border. And they found the going good and the plunder
plenty. They had swarmed across from Las Cuevas, down

below Laredo, in droves of from fifty to one hundred. One band had struck through Duval County up toward Beeville, and Buck Pettus had his vigilantes in the saddle.

Two or maybe three bands of twenty-five or more had struck toward Goliad and Refugio, where Hines Clark and Martin Culver gathered up their vigilantes and turned them back.

Mike Dunn and two neighbor ranchers, Jim Lane and John Wilson, had surrendered when about thirty outlaws swarmed into their cow camp one evening up on the south bank of the Nueces River. For some reason or another the bandits held them as hostages for about a week, then pushed them out in front on one of their big raids—on Tom Noakes' store at Nuecestown.

That raid made Nueces history for two or three reasons. It was the farthest inland the river bandits had struck in force. It was pulled off on a religious holiday—Good Friday, March 26, 1875. And the bandits took eighteen brand-new Dick Heye saddles, which were what you'd call now the Cadillacs of the saddle world. They were heavily studded with silver conchos in a pattern you could tell half a mile away, a fact that proved to be the death warrant for many a man.

The day before the Captain took the outfit into Corpus, the people had hung a bandit on a big pecan tree at the edge of the plaza. He had been brought in by Pat Whelan, who'd been out scouting with an eight-man posse when they raised a small bandit outfit on the Little Oso. Pat had lost two men and killed three bandits, and brought one in.

From Sheriff McClure, Pat Whelan, and Mike Dunn, Captain got a good picture of the situation right away. From Dunn he got a full report on the Nuecestown raid: Tom Noakes, who ran the big store there, took the five Noakes children through a tunnel he'd built to the river, but Noakes' wife, Martha, had tried to save her feather bed from the burning store and had been quirted and mistreated. Things like that sure riled the Captain.

Captain seemed mighty concerned about those eighteen Dick Heye saddles. He got Mike Dunn to give him a good picture of them—length of the tapideros, if the skirts were conchoed. He wanted all details. He also asked Mike to describe the man who quirted Martha Noakes. Mike told him he was a two-pistoled American dressed in all the mail-order finery. "Some taller than usual," Mike added. "Brown —saddle-colored—hair. Had a heavy, deep scar, reaching from his hairline to the point of his chin, on the right side. One of those regular rowdy dudes. He was trying to make Martha tell him where the money box was hid. But she was the spunkiest woman I ever saw. She wouldn't drop her feather bed, and she wouldn't tell him nothing. He laid his quirt down her back mighty heavy."

Sol Lichtenstein, owner of the biggest store in Corpus, was standing by Captain while Mike talked. "Captain," Sol said, "I got some of those saddles on order, but they ain't in yet or I'd show you one."

Captain studied a minute, then told Sol, "When they come, don't sell a one until I tell you differently." He turned to Sergeant Armstrong and ordered, "Describe those saddles to the Rangers. Make sure they understand exactly. Then order them to empty those saddles on sight. No palavering with the riders. Empty them. Leave the men where you drop them, and bring the saddles to camp."

This order later on got Captain in quite some trouble at Austin, and it was talked about a whole lot in the governor's campaign. But I can say for sure, after all these years, there wasn't a man shot out of a Dick Heye saddle who wasn't down in The Book.

Captain chewed on the butt of his unlit cigar for some

time, and then he faced Old Sol and said, "The Legislature didn't give me a dime, but I've got to have supplies. Rifles, mainly. Ammunition, and a few victuals. I'll—"

Sol took him by the arm and led him toward his store, saying somewhat proudly, "There's the biggest store, the best stock of supplies, 'twixt Santone and Brownsville. Come in. Pick out what you want. All you want."

"You might not get paid," Captain warned. "The carpet-baggers didn't leave much money in Austin, and the boys up there ain't willing to spend any of it to stop what they call a war in this Nueces country."

"I'll do the worrying," Old Sol said. "It's better for me to give you my stock than it is for those river bandits to come in and get it. Take what you want and sign a receipt." Leading Captain into the store, Sol continued, "Tom Noakes would've done that if you'd got here in time. You betcha."

Then Old Sol grinned. "Now, about rifles," he said, "you're in plumb luck, Captain. We got a big shipment by the last boat from the east. All the latest model repeaters— Henrys, Spencers, Winchesters—"

"How about Sharps?" Captain asked.

"Sharps? Sure, we always carry a small stock for the buffalo hunters. Maybe thirty or so—"

"I want them," Captain said.

"Sharps, Captain? I thought you were going man hunting—not buffalo. Those heavy, single-shot Sharps—whew! When you hit a buffalo, he's yours. If you miss, you can reload. If you miss a man—"

"I don't want men who miss," Captain said.

Old Sol had thirty-six Sharps carbines. Captain took them. They were boogers. I broke mine open and that fifty-caliber bore looked big enough for a gopher to crawl through. That flat-nosed bullet looked as big as your thumb. It was plenty wicked. But—no second chance.

As time went on I came to know that right there was Captain's idea of fighting. He gave you one big chance; then you were on your own. You learned mighty quick not to bust that cap till you had your target lined up in your sights. Naturally, I had never handled a gun that big and heavy. But like most any other country boy of that time, I was a fair-to-middling shot with either a rifle or pistol. And I was quick to learn from the older hands.

Old Sol stocked our wagon with box after box of pistol and rifle shells and a good supply of parched coffee, frijoles, and corn meal.

Pat Whelan was the last man Captain talked to before he lined us out of Corpus to the west an hour or so before sundown. He ordered Pat to disband his posses and to notify all the others he saw to do the same thing, except when they were deputized and under command of Sheriff McClure.

"I'll try," Pat promised.

"I said nothing about trying," Captain explained coldly. "I ordered you to disband them."

Pat hedged some. "All of them may not want to disband."

"That's right," Captain said. "Some of them don't. They're the ones who have a little private killing to do in the name of a posse. But I want you to notify all that, beginning now, armed bands picked up in public will be treated as outlaws."

"We'll be glad to help you, Captain—"

"When I want you to help me," Captain said sharplike, "I'll put you on my roster. Give you a full-time job. Hunting outlaws is a good, full-time job. That's what we've been hired to do. Get that word to all these posses."

Meeting Captain King

We rode maybe an hour in a brisk walk. Then we rode into the fringe of a rain squall, one of the sort that happens only along the Texas coast. It was the first one I had seen or been in. The skies closed in and almost blotted out the setting sun, and the wind gusted around from all directions, it appeared.

As a farm boy I admired the good spring season and green fields all along the Texas coast. There was moisture aplenty, and this rain squall was only extra. By dark water was standing on flat ground that didn't seem to drain in any direction.

That made the going heavy for our column. Anybody who hasn't been in this coast country before they built roads couldn't have any idea of how boggy the black ground gets when it's well soaked. It doesn't seem to have any bottom, and even the snipes get bogged.

Dad Smith had rigged up a light farm wagon with bows and a tarp. It wasn't too heavy loaded with supplies, but it got so it could move only a short distance before that black, sticky gumbo had to be cleaned off the wheels. Dad's wagon was hooked to a well-matched span of mules that could pull almost anything loose at both ends, except when their every step sunk them in better than hock deep and they had to pull out one foot at a time.

We weren't making any distance, but there wasn't any place to pull up for a halt. To stop in that mire meant you'd only sink deeper, and Captain kept us moving.

This being the second straight night we'd been in the saddle, neither men nor mounts were in very good shape. My old nag was a good, solid farm horse with plenty of chest and bottom, but he got so near fagged that I had to rowel him just about every step.

It was well past daylight when, on ahead, we saw a ground swell. It was packed with beeves, deer, jackrabbits —and rattlesnakes, as we soon found out. A funny thing about animals and snakes: in weather like this they get along, side by side.

The sun came up bright and hot; the sky was clear and blue; and this swell seemed to be the far edge of the rain belt. Just beyond it a bit was a wooden trestle spanning the Little Oso. We had covered something like twelve miles since leaving Corpus.

Maben and Parrott, scouting ahead, waved Captain up and showed him two Mexicans dangling from the trestle. They'd been hung several days before. Captain shook his head, Maben later told me, and flushed red with anger. "Outlaws didn't do that," he said. "Some posseman worked off an old grudge."

Captain didn't halt us or turn us onto that high ground. Up ahead he found the footing more solid, and he waved the column on. When we had crossed the trestle, he didn't give us any new orders—he showed us what to do. He dismounted, loosened his saddle cinches, lashed his heavy pistol belt across his saddle, and marched ahead—afoot, leading his mount.

The rest of did the same. I was as hungry as a country boy could be. And I didn't have a scabbard for my Sharps. Like a greenhorn I had cradled it all night in the crook of my arm. One of the older hands showed me how to lash it with saddle thongs in a bow knot that would drop it loose easy.

Captain perked all of us up, just showing us. I forgot about being hungry. Good bright sun, good-smelling fresh air—and me, a strapping youngster only being asked to do what a little preacherish-looking Captain did. If I grumbled or let him outdo me I'd better have stayed on the farm.

The column didn't make any speed, but we got to Banquette by midafternoon and Captain put us into camp. In no time at all Dad Smith had a good fire going and a pot of frijoles under way. He dumped a double handful of parched coffee in some boiling water, and it wasn't long till we all had a cup of it and some biscuits that must have been made up before Dad left East Texas. But when they were soaked they went down mighty easy.

We hobbled our horses and choused them out to the wrangler to graze. We were at home now, joshing around like we were at a Sunday foot-washing.

Banquette in those days was quite a place, even though it had only one inhabitant—that being old W6 Wright. One of him was enough—more population than most places.

Before the Americans swarmed over the place Banquette had been a sort of a frolic center for the Mexicans. They came in for their Saturday night *bailes*; and of course on feast days they had their horse shows, roping contests, and rooster fights. They also had a little adobe chapel where they prayed.

It was by now more of a ghost town, mostly in ruins. The stock pens were only outlines of broken-down stockades and fences. The little one-room chapel still had a roof of sorts, but it was chipped and chunked off nearly to ruins. Still, it was the only thing that looked like a shelter of any sort.

Banquette was known then, and for some years more, as the jumping-off place into the lower Nueces country. At the time Captain McNelly came in it was pretty well known as the sheriff's deadline. Men on the dodge figured if they made Banquette they could make the Rio Grande without too much trouble from the law.

Folks who started the stage line from San Antonio to Brownsville tried to make a remount station there, but they couldn't keep any stock. The stagecoaches now stopped only when they had a package to leave off for some of the ranchers in the area. These were left in care of old W6 to deliver when he could.

Nobody knew where old W6 came from, because nobody asked. You didn't ask such questions. It wasn't polite, and it was sort of risky. Where a man was from and what his maiden name was before coming to Texas was reckoned as his own affair.

I heard later that old W6 dropped in from nowhere— started burning W6 on steer flanks and claiming everything in sight, including five or six sections of mighty good grazing land lying along the south bank of the Nueces. He claimed he won the land with his thirty-thirty Winchester.

He was a talky old booger and would lay a bet on anything under the sun. Whether the stagecoach would get through to Brownsville with all its passengers and baggage, and so on. You name it and choose sides.

"Howdy, Cap," he gabbed at Captain. "Heading for the lower country?"

"Maybe," Captain shot back.

"How many hands you got?"

"Forty-two."

"Betcha a hundred you don't take forty-two in with you all the way,"

"I don't bet," Captain said.

"Betcha a hundred you don't bring twenty out."

"I don't bet," Captain said shortlike and turned to walk away.

Old W6 took Captain by the arm and said, "Wait a minute, Cap," and pointed to the old chapel. "The stage driver yesterday left a box of books for me to give you. Government books—from the governor. They're right over there in the casita. Come along. I'll show you."

He lifted out a sizable box with the lid pried off. "I thought they were mail-order catalogs at first. But they ain't. They're names of some of our citizens who appear to have been in trouble back home. A passel of 'em."

Captain took one of the books and began thumbing the pages.

"I ain't in there," W6 said. "I already looked; else I'd be across the river by this time."

All of us Rangers ringed close around, gawking. I was sure curious. The book looked as big as a mail-order catalog. The greenhorn in me got the upper hand, and I blurted out, "Is that book full of names, Captain? What are they—?" Captain scorched me down with a blistering look, and Corporal Rudd nudged me back.

Captain handed one each to Lieutenants Wright and Robinson and Sergeants Armstrong and Orrill. He kept one for himself, then ordered the box to be thrown in the wagon.

Some of the older hands who had worked for Captain before guessed that this was a list of men wanted for crimes all over the country, men whose last-known address since the war was Texas. They said it was a list made up by Captain when he worked awhile for the Republicans right after the war, setting up a State Police. He worked less than a year and then quit when he saw they aimed to take law-enforcement into their own hands and not let the people have any say.

Now that the Democrats had run the carpetbaggers out and were in power in Austin, they had printed that list in the book. The older hands with us reckoned the Governor had ordered Captain to handle them.

A little while by sun, Sergeant Orrill whistled us into company line and formed us for overnight camp. I had caught a couple of catnaps since we got to Banquette, but I was sleepy—and my turn on guard wouldn't come until the third posting.

The next morning our mounts were pretty well freshened up; and as for me, I was loaded with frijoles up to my ears and feeling like a country boy ought to feel at the beginning of a new day.

Captain had huddled considerably with his officers and old W6 and made his decision as to which way to move the outfit on this morning. Some of the bandits who had raided through the Nueces and Goliad country had headed back for the river at Las Cuevas with several cartloads of hides and other loot from the settlements.

A bigger band had turned down the coast from Banquette. Those bandits were loaded with plunder, including

most of the Dick Heye saddles. They no doubt would take a
fling at high society in Brownsville and Matamoros, and
show off all their finery.

So Captain headed the outfit down the coast after he had
formed us and moved us out along the old Taylor trail—
named after General Taylor of the Mexican War. This trail
skirted the edge of the Big Sands, an area of sand dunes
between the present cities of Falfurrias and Edinburg,
through country fairly well open.

But we moved at the ready. Captain had flank riders well
out in front. Every Ranger had his pistol belt plumb full of
cartridges, and five of those big Sharps shells in his pocket.
At least that's where I had mine, because they wouldn't fit
into my pistol belt.

Captain moved us at only a brisk walk. He seemed to
know exactly where he was going and what he was up to.
Two or three times he pulled aside from the front and
waited for the wagon to come up, and he had some talk
with Dad Smith. But he wasn't wound up, and he wasn't
chewing on the butt of his cigar.

We moved for about two days, doing nothing much but
traveling. Then, a couple of hours by sun, we pulled up at
Santa Gertrudis. This was a town with more than a hundred people, on Captain Richard King's ranch of the same
name.

At that time Santa Gertrudis had been established a little
more than twenty years. The main ranch house was centered with a steeple, maybe seventy-five feet high. And it
was manned by two lookouts.

They had picked us up way out yonder, and their scouts
had hurried out to have a closer look. They piloted us into
the outer area of the cluster of buildings, and Captain King
rode out and took over.

This was, of course, the first time I had laid eyes on Cap-

Ranger Captain Lee McNelly. His appearance was gentle, his courage boundless; and his brilliant leadership of a small group of men tamed the wild Nueces Strip.

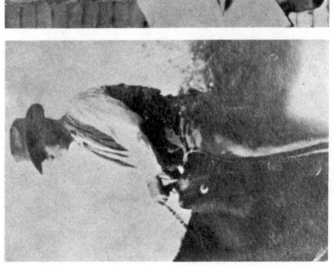

George Durham. Becoming a "McNelly Ranger" while still a teen-age youth newly arrived from Georgia, he carried that designation, proudly, as a young man (left) and as an old man (right), and to his grave. (Courtesy Robert C. Wells, the King Ranch)

tain Richard King. And like Captain McNelly, he wasn't too much to look at the first time. In fact, he was a dead-ringer for Captain McNelly at a short distance. Each of them hefted around 130 or 135, stood about five and a half feet, had brown hair and beards. Neither of them looked like a storybook captain of anything. But they were. Both of them.

Most of the stock pens and traps at Santa Gertrudis were built of lumber. Sawed lumber. I learned later that Captain King and Captain Mifflin Kenedy had swapped a boatload of steers for a boatload of sawed lumber from Florida. Both had come to Texas from back East during the Mexican War, then had run river steamers for Charley Stillman during the gold-rush days when swarms of folks landed at Brownsville on their way to California. They had started the Santa Gertrudis as partners in the middle fifties, but had begun dividing up four or five years before we arrived. They had come back from the Rio Grande as far as they could, to get away from the river raiders and the Cortinistas. They had managed to brand many a longhorn, but they hadn't managed to keep the raiders away.

The Santa Gertrudis ranch house was more like an army arsenal inside. In one big room there were eighty stands of Henry repeating rifles and maybe a hundred boxes of shells. Two men stood in the lookout tower day and night, and there was always a man at the ready for each of those rifles. But that didn't stop the raiders.

When we unsaddled and penned our horses Captain King looked them over and shook his head.

"How in the world did you get this far on those nags?" he asked Captain McNelly. "You must have had to walk some."

"They're all we had," Captain McNelly said, "and the main fact is—we're here."

We were put up for the night. There were bunks for all who wanted to bed down inside. There was good beef aplenty, and we got the best—some of the best beef stew I ever greased my chin with, it seemed. And the coffee—well, I drank plenty. It was good. It would have been good in any country, but the way they served it here at Santa Gertrudis, I overdid it.

We ate in the grub shanty. Only it wasn't a shanty—it was a hall with four tables seating maybe a hundred. We filed by and filled our mess kits and got a cup of coffee. A woman and a young girl gave us refills whenever we needed them. I soon found out that by emptying my coffee cup this girl would come up, reach across my shoulder, and say "Could I pour you some more?" I would have drunk cup after cup of coyote poison if she'd have refilled for me. Three times I said, "If you don't mind, ma'm," and three times I said, "Thank you, ma'm."

Whenever she walked up it seemed like somebody had dumped over the lilac water. I reckon I'd have sat there and drunk coffee till it ran out of my ears, but she seemed to catch on after awhile and didn't come back to me.

I struck up a little talk with one of the stock hands and found that the girl's name was the only name under the sun it could have been—Caroline. Somehow I knew it had to be Caroline. And she was a niece of Captain King's wife. She was Caroline Chamberlain.

I bedded down out in the open saddle shed, but I didn't go to sleep. That coffee was biling me from foot to head— and my head was spinning like a squirrel cage, but not only from the coffee. I decided not to leave this place. I'd pull out from Captain McNelly and hire on here as a ranch hand. I'd work hard till I got to be a foreman; then I'd ask Caroline to marry me. Only a country boy could have had such crazy ideas. Maybe the three-quarter moon also had something to do with it.

I finally dozed off around daylight, and was shaken to my feet by Corporal Rudd. Our nags were gone and the pen was full of some real saddle horses. The others were picking out their mounts, dropping a loop on them easy-like and hauling them in.

I had a lariat rope, all right, but I don't know what for. I had aimed to practice when I got the chance, but right then I couldn't have looped a post. And Caroline was right down there in the corral, as much at home as she'd been in the mess hall! What to do I didn't know, but I sure did give up any idea of trying to go to work as a ranch hand.

Captain King then proved he could read men better than he could read the back of his hand. He spoke to one of his vaqueros, who dropped a rope on a good, rangy sorrel gelding and brought him up. Captain King said, friendlylike, "Where you from, son?" I told him Georgia. Then he asked, "How come you to hire on with Captain McNelly?"

I told him my father had worked for Captain during the war. He nodded, again friendlylike. He examined my old saddle. The cotton cords in the cinch were worn thin and one was all but gone. It had no skirt—and the stirrups were the thin, wooden kind, and well worn. It was a cheap farm saddle to begin with, and it had begun many years ago.

He told his vaquero to give me another saddle and a rifle scabbard. I never forgot that.

I reckon he looked just once at me and knew I never could rope me a mount. Looking back through the years I see how crazy a country boy could get—planning to leave the Rangers and go to work for Captain King as a ranch hand. In the first place, of course, if I had left Captain Mc-Nelly there, Captain King wouldn't have let me stay all night on the ranch. I never had a crazier idea—or was it? I finally worked it out, all right. I got to be a foreman, and—but that all comes later. I didn't quit Captain McNelly until he was in his grave.

At that time I must have been the shabbiest looker in the outfit. None of the others were dudes, but they wore good hats and boots. Their clothes were worn, but mine were worn and shabby to start with. My hat was skimpy and limber. In fact, it had served my dad for a good many years—and was a cheap farm hat to start with. My britches were homespun jeans, patched in the seat, and I had long ago outgrown them. My boots were farmer's boots—square-toed, with some of the hair still on them. But I was healthy and husky, and willing to learn. And I was dead set to make good with Captain, to go where he sent me and do what he told me to.

When I cinched the saddle on that sorrel gelding he made a picture, and I had to step back and look him over. Back home, he and that saddle would have been worth at least two hundred dollars. The horse had a good, roomy chest, open flanks, wide nostrils. He had some good breeding. But I was just looking.

"You like him, son?" I turned and saw Captain King right behind me, smiling. I could only nod my head for "yes."

"How much is a horse like that worth, Captain?"

He gave me a little smile and said, "Don't let that bother you, son. Wherever Captain McNelly sends you that horse will take you. He's a good, solid animal. Plenty of stay, and enough speed." I was a happy youngun.

Most of the other hands were now saddled, but Captain McNelly had not picked his horse. His eye was roving over the milling pen. You could tell he was following a big bay, a standout even in that pen.

"That's Segal. You want him?" Captain King asked,

again proving he seemed to see everything and to savvy men.

Captain McNelly nodded his head slowly. "That's a five-hundred-dollar horse. What a piece of horse flesh! I couldn't ask you for that animal. Texas would never pay you for him."

Then Captain King said the same thing Old Sol had said back in Corpus: "I'd rather give him to you than have those bandits come and take him. Most of those rascals are mounted on my stock, and I at least want to do as good by you, Captain."

As we pulled away from Santa Gertrudis we were a lot different outfit from the motley crew that Captain had flung together only a week ago back at Burton. We were forted and ready for anything.

For myself, I felt mighty chesty. For the first time in my life I had a prime bit of horse flesh between my knees, and that always does something to a man. We all had good rifles, good pistols, and we were behind a leader who didn't bobble or look back—a leader who had done nothing but win, a leader that the governor was betting on to bring law to the Nueces Strip.

In Bandit Country

As we moved out we naturally fell into our places in the line like a trained military outfit. We were single file and about five spaces apart. I was third back from Corporal Rudd. You could feel something in that fresh morning air.

Captain was at the front of the column, and astraddle of that big bay he looked like a captain. All our mounts were good, but none could touch Segal.

We moved at a brisk canter, with a patrol well out front and flank riders on both sides.

The first thing I noticed out of the usual was when I smelled smoke. Not camp smoke—more like the heavy smoke from a burned building. And that was what it proved to be. In a little while we passed the charred remains of what had been the buildings at Rancho la Parra. It couldn't have been more than twenty-four hours or so since it was burned.

And then we saw, well out front, Sergeant Armstrong gallop into the clear, circle with his right arm twice, and let his hand fall to the south. He had sighted somebody.

Captain McNelly stopped and waved a signal to his officers. The three corporals ahead moved their men to the left. Corporal Rudd and the others moved to the right. It was all done like it might have been practiced for a long time. It had been, of course, but back in war days. I didn't savvy the move, being one of the few who hadn't fought in the war. But I stayed third man back from Rudd and halted five paces to his right in a line that formed a half moon.

Captain lifted his pistol, twirled the chamber, tested the trigger action, and dropped the pistol back in the holster. We all did the same.

Sergeant Armstrong and Jim Wofford took positions on each side of the trail, well out in the open and in plain sight of the outfit. Then a body of men came up, bunched, in a disorderly formation.

It turned out to be Hines Clark and Martin Culver with their joint posse. Armstrong and Wofford led them up to Captain McNelly. Later on I got a word-by-word report on what took place, and I want to pass it along for the first time. There's been lots of talk through the years of trades and dickers, but here's the way it actually was.

Culver spurred ahead as spokesman for the posse. When he came up to Captain he was all smiles and, friendlylike, said, "Captain, we got about a hundred men. All white men. Nary a Yankee, nigger, or Mexican amongst us—"

"Did you overhaul the raiders?" Captain cut in.

"No, we didn't. They got plumb away. Got back across the river."

Captain studied a minute, putting an unlit cigar in his mouth.

Culver said, "We're going to pitch in and help you, Captain."

"I've got all the men I need," Captain replied. "I'm going to disband and disarm these men and return them to their homes."

"They won't do that," Culver said.

"Then I'm ordering you to. Disband and disarm them."

"They won't do that for me," Culver said.

"They will for me," Captain shot back, chewing hard on his cigar butt, a sign we soon learned meant Captain was wound up and on the prod.

Culver weakened some and said, "We'll have to vote on that. Then we'll let you know."

"You'll have ten minutes to take that vote. If you don't vote to lay down those arms and surrender to the regular law of Texas, my Rangers will move on you and lay them down for you."

"Meaning we're the same as outlaws?" Culver bristled.

"I can't prove you are right now. I don't know what all you posses have been doing. But at the end of ten minutes you will be—you'll be reckoned as armed outlaws. And we've been sent in to kill them."

Captain had his watch in his left hand and was glancing down at it regular. As the time played out he lifted his pistol, and every other Ranger pistol cleared leather.

One of the posse moved out alone, rode up to Captain, and handed him his pistol, butt forward. Captain holstered his pistol and told the posseman, "You may keep it. But use it only to defend your home."

And that's about the way it happened. When that first

posseman rode up and surrendered his pistol—that was when Captain McNelly took over the Nueces country in the name of regular constituted law. At least, the regular law took root there by demanding respect and obedience.

Lots of people who weren't there still claim that Captain McNelly was bluffing. Not a single man who was there, or who came to know Captain McNelly, believes that way. Captain never did flinch, never did bluff. When he gave an order he expected quick and total obedience, and he didn't give an order until he was ready to enforce it.

Those possemen single-filed by and halted until Captain nodded them on. I doubt if there was ever another peace officer who could have turned that trick. But I'll set down now my experience, after more than fifty years as a peace officer: People respect an officer if he's fit to respect.

When the outfit moved again we were more fanned out and readied. Corporal Rudd took three of his dab and moved up to the right and wide, spaced at about 150 paces. The country wasn't too heavy-brushed then—mostly oak motts in dense clusters, or sort of brush islands, surrounded by open spaces.

This was, of course, my first time working the brush; but I knew by the way we were being handled that we were coming into outlaw country, and that you'd better not get out in one of those clearings till you knew what was in the motts.

We guided off Corporal Rudd. A little after sundown he motioned us in and we soon came up to the main body of Rangers. Captain was putting us in dry camp in a big ten-acre mott, known as Mota Tablon. It was located eight or so miles above the present city of Raymondville, and you could have lost a hundred hands and horses in it.

No fires were made. No coffee. No nothing. I was fast learning to skip mealtime. But I knew Captain was skipping every meal the hands skipped, and that kept me from getting too hungry.

They doubled our guard to eight hands in three shifts for the night. I bedded down like an old-timer, on my saddle right behind my big sorrel, and slept sound till I was shaken awake to take my turn on guard.

After daylight Dad Smith fired up and soon had coffee, corn pone, and plenty of good, sliced side meat fried in corn meal. He had got several hundred pounds of salt pork at the Santa Gertrudis, and it sure put a good bottom in a man's stomach.

After we had eaten, Captain ordered us up for a roll call. While we were lined up he walked up and down before us, giving us a talk.

"We're now in outlaw country," he said, "and you'll be ordered out in scouting patrols of twos and threes. There are only two kinds of people for us—outlaws and law-abiding. Treat these law-abiding folks with all respect, regardless of color or size. Don't enter a house unless the man invites you in. Don't take a roasting ear or melon unless he tells you to. If his dog barks at you, get away from it. Don't shoot it. Let them know we're their friends sent down to help them.

"As for the others: Place under arrest and bring into camp everybody else. Horseback or afoot, singly or in groups. Arrest them, fetch them into camp.

"Until further orders, all prisoners will be put under the old Spanish law—*la ley de fuga*—which means the prisoner is to be killed on the spot if a rescue is attempted.

"Now—any questions Anybody got anything to say?"

A man in Polly Williams' dab stepped forward, looking at the ground, and finally stammered, "Captain, this plans to be longer than I figured. I got some stock I better look after—"

"You want a discharge?" Captain half-snarled.

"I reckon so."

Captain was ready. He seemed to know what would happen. He pulled some papers from the inside pocket of his jacket, scribbled on one of them, and handed it to Lieutenant Robinson. "Scratch him off," he ordered; and the man got a discharge showing five days service.

Four more stepped out and got their discharges.

"Turn in your rifles and any other state property you might have," he ordered. "I'm going to ask you, but I can't force you, to go back out by the Santa Gertrudis and swap back for your old nags."

Then the Captain gave each of the rest of us one copy of The Book. "If you have any trouble bringing a man in and have to leave him, try to identify him from these names in this book and scratch him."

The Book was a dinger. As I recollect, it had 228 pages, filled solid with names and descriptions. Some names had two lines of type, some had eight in big black type. Those, we were told, were the swapouts—men who wouldn't be taken prisoner. They were wanted for all sorts of crimes in most every state, north and south. There were upwards of five thousand of them.

"These outlaws," Captain said when all those books were handed out, "have been running roughshod over decent folks—burning, plundering, raiding, murdering. They claim to be bigger than the law—bigger than the United States law, bigger than Texas and Texas law. It's up to us to see if they're right or if they're wrong. We've got fighting to do. But I'll never send you into a fight. I'll lead you in.

"Any questions? Anybody got anything to say?"

No more men stepped out, and Captain nodded to Lieutenant Robinson to get us under way.

From Mota Tablon we veered west, at the ready, with

four scouts well in advance and flank riders spread wide. We had pulled off the Taylor trail for a mile or so when we saw one of the scouts, Deaf Rector, ride out in a sendaro, wave a signal, and drop his hand to the south. He had spotted another body of men. Again the signal came down and we all froze where we were.

Rector and Ranger Adams piloted a column of men back to the Captain, and it turned out to be Captain Coldwell and his Ranger company. By military telegraph Austin had ordered him out of the section for duty in the upper country.

Naturally, he wasn't too friendly with Captain McNelly. But bringing him out and sending McNelly in wasn't as bad as some have tried to make it look. Coldwell and his men made a great record against the Indians on the northwest frontier of Texas, but Coldwell just wasn't the man to handle those Nueces outlaws. No more than the military. Coldwell tried to fight according to the books as written in Austin. The military had to fight by the books as written in Washington. But those Nueces outlaws didn't fight by any books. Neither did Captain McNelly. They made their own rules, and Captain made his. They didn't mind killing. Neither did Captain McNelly. They didn't take prisoners. Neither did Captain McNelly.

"What's good enough for those outlaws is good enough for me," Captain McNelly explained as to why he put prisoners under *la ley de fuga*. But I want to go on record now: I never did agree with that harsh law. It's too brutal. But those were orders.

Captain McNelly was no stranger to that lower country. He had tried to help the Republicans set up civil law during reconstruction days, but when he saw they didn't really want to he quit them. I found out later that in 1872, when the U. S. Congress sent down a commission to look into the lawlessness along the Rio Grande, Captain McNelly worked for them, bringing in witnesses. I've seen the report he wrote at that time. It went something like this:

Many of these border citizens have not nerve enough to take an active, decided stand, either by giving information or personal assistance. A number of them have done it for me and some ten or twelve have paid with their lives. It is the history of this border when a citizen gives information or helps fight raiders, he has been forced to move out or pay with his life. There is a large floating population on this side who work as spies for Cortinas. . . .

Captain estimated that more than 2,000 ranchers and other citizens had been killed by raiders and more than 900,000 head of stock stolen; yet there was no record of any raider ever paying the penalty for his crime through regular court procedures. The military and the Rangers had arrested them in droves, only to see them released in a day or so to go back to their deviltry.

I want to put this down to answer those people who have called Captain mean things all these years. With nothing but a commission from the governor, and without a dime of cash or even supplies, he was sent in to do a job that all others had failed to do and that had to be done if that Nueces Strip was ever to be livable for law-abiding folks.

I repeat that Neal Coldwell was a good Ranger and had a good outfit, but those bandits raided above him and below him. Lots of them surrendered to him, though, and he fooled away his time taking them to jail, only to see them make bond and get out before his hands got their horses watered and fed.

"These bandit gangs are too smart and too well organized," Coldwell now told McNelly. "They've got spies everywhere. They know where every soldier and every

Ranger outfit is, and they know your moves before you can make them. They're bigger and smarter than the law."

Captain seemed to change his plans for us after talking to Coldwell. He reasoned—right—that the bandit spies knew about Coldwell being ordered out. And he took a chance on them not knowing we had been sent in.

After Coldwell left, moving up the Taylor trail, Captain pulled us back a mile or so and planted us in some motts a couple of miles north of the ranch buildings at Rancho los Indios. He hid us like a cow hides a newborn calf and left us all day, except for the patrols he kept roving under the best cover available.

That night I had just dozed off when the guard came down the line, shook every shoulder, and whispered the command to get ready to move.

It couldn't have been much more than five minutes when we had formed our line, in twos, out in the open with hardly enough moonlight to make a shadow. Lieutenant Wright was in charge and moved us out behind him. We moved cautious all night, cut the Taylor trail farther down, and at daybreak went into dry camp in some motts right near a spring in a willow grove—from which El Sauz got its name, and which was later my home.

Captain again holed us up close all day, but he had some of his older hands making wide scouts in singles and pairs.

Then the word got around that a strange man was riding with Captain McNelly. This turned out to be J. S. Rock, a famous Brownsville scout who had worked with Captain McNelly during the time he was down here with the men from Congress. None of us knew at the time, of course, that it was Old Rock. We didn't even know then who Old Rock was. But we knew something was building up.

Then I drew my first lookout detail. Sergeant Orrill showed me my station—a small mott on a little ground swell, with a view of open country for some distance. We concealed my mount in the brush and he told me to climb the highest mesquite and keep a lookout.

"If I see anyone, then what?" I asked schoolkidlike.

Old Sarge just grinned and said, "Orders are to bring them to camp, son."

"If there are more than one?" I asked.

"Son, orders are orders. Bring them into camp."

I had been in my post an hour or so when my field glasses picked up a rider, quite a bit to the east, coming into the Taylor trail. I shinnied down, and I was somewhat nervous. This was to be my first catch. My jitters sort of went to the horse, and I wrestled him around quite a bit before I got aboard. I was to find out pretty quick that a nervous man makes a nervous horse. A cool man makes a cool horse.

I flew across the opening in a long lope and overhauled my man. He turned out to be a dressed-up Mex riding a mule. I couldn't *habla* Mex and he couldn't *habla* United States. He wanted to argue by heaving up his shoulders and jabbering and turning up his palms to me. So I finally shoved my pistol in his ribs and pointed, and he got the idea.

In camp our interpreter, McGovern, got his story. The Mex was on his way to get married—the padre and the gal were waiting at the chapel at Los Indios. But McGovern told him that was too damn bad. That wedding would have to wait. They gave him a good frisk, but he had nothing. He was warned not to try to escape, and then turned loose in camp. He made a pretty handy man for Dad Smith.

Before I went back to my lookout, Ranger Matt Fleming came into camp piloting a rider who was still armed and not under arrest. He had turned up right before Fleming and had asked to be brought to the Captain.

I barely got a look at the man's face, but what I saw

made me want to look again. He wore a straggly red beard flecked with white, and red hair dropping almost to his shoulders. His skin was dry and parched, and his light-blue eyes seemed to throw off sparks. He was what you would call spooky.

He was old Jesus Sandoval. He looked like a crazy man—and that was what he was: a man who had lost a wife and daughter to the bandits and who now lived for the sole purpose of killing them.

Both Captain and Old Rock had worked with him, had used him, and knew him. Captain put him on the payroll that day. Jesus Sandoval became our jailer, and he never lost a single one that was turned over to him for keeping.

Men like Old Rock and Jesus (or Casoose) fit into Captain's plans like a glove on the hand. Captain made his record in the war handling a hundred-man guerilla band in Louisiana, and he knew the value of a good spy system.

Rock wasn't a killer. That is, he didn't live just to kill bandits. Old Casoose did. But both men knew every cow trail, every crossing on the river.

Captain spent most of the day in the saddle with Old Rock, and they covered a pretty wide area scouting for signs. He ordered all patrols in for roll call that evening and gave us another pep talk.

"We've had two good men join up with us," he said, pointing. "Old Rock here, and Casoose. They know every trail and they'll take us to where the shooting is good. If two or more of you flush out some bandits, whether they're running or forted and holed up, put yourselves at five-pace intervals and shoot only at the target right in front of you. Don't shoot to the left or the right. Shoot straight ahead. And don't shoot till you've got your target good in your sights.

"Don't walk up on a wounded man. Pay no attention to a

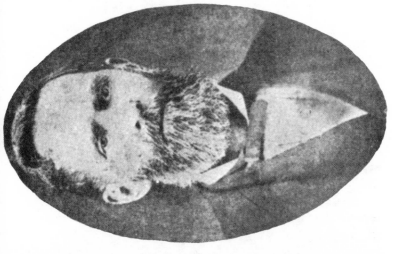
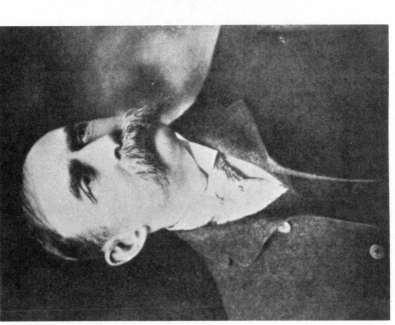

John Armstrong (left) and Henry Clay Pleasants (right). Armstrong was the first sergeant of Captain McNelly's Ranger company; Pleasants served as judge of the Twenty-third District during the Sutton-Taylor feud.

King Fisher (upper left), John Wesley Hardin (upper right), and Juan Nepomucino Cortinas (below). They were among the thousands of men who made Captain McNelly's task unbelievably difficult. Fisher reigned over his own kingdom in Southwest Texas. The notorious Hardin was a killer who claimed at least twenty victims. Cortinas, who was for a time governor of Tamaulipas, Mexico, initially licensed many of the cattle rustlers who roamed the Nueces Strip.

white flag. That's a mean trick bandits use on green hands.
Don't touch a dead man except to identify him. And treat
the law-abiding people with respect."

Captain spoke in a weak, thin voice that didn't carry very
far. But I knew now that his voice, like his looks, was mis-
leading, because I knew a lot more about the man than
when I first saw him. He was a consumptive who had come
to Texas from his native Virginia when a lad of fifteen or
thereabouts. His folks had had him in school to be a
preacher. In Texas he hadn't had much time to rest and
cure his consumption. When war broke out he joined up
with the 5th Texas Cavalry. In Louisiana he served more
than four years without a day's sick leave, we now knew.
He was made a captain and given a hundred guerilla
scouts to handle.

After the war he married and tried to set up cotton farming on a soldier's headright in Washington County. He quit
his farm for about a year to help the reconstruction Republicans set up a State Police. When he saw they didn't aim
to help civil law, as I said, he quit.

He worked some for a citizens' group in Karnes and De-
Witt counties, trying to calm down that Taylor-Sutton
feud. But things were so rowdy they couldn't hold a district court, and Captain figured he didn't have authority to
do anything but make arrests, so he left that work.

Then he became a marshal at La Grange and worked for
the congressional committee. He never did find time to
cure his consumption by staying on the farm and having
his wife, Carrie, cook good grub and taking it easylike,
which is the only way to cure consumption.

When he talked to us Rangers, as he was now doing, you
could barely hear him down the line. He sure didn't look
like a fighting man. His brown hair was fine and silky, and
he let it hang down long. His beard was also fine and silky

—it came down to his chest. He dressed neat as a pin—wore a good grade beaver hat, duck pants and brush jacket, soft calf-skin leggings, a hand-tooled pistol belt, and a pistol with a horn grip.

I never have yet figured out what there was about the Captain that worked such a spell over his hands. When and how he put on his iron control over this outfit I didn't know —and still don't. When he spoke we hardly breathed. Leastwise, I didn't. Even the horses seemed to quit swishing and stomping.

While the night was young we broke camp and moved, at the ready, to the south below Laguna Larga, then swung west toward the Rio Grande. In the dim light of a first-quarter moon we moved well bunched, with scouts, led by Old Rock, not too far ahead. Rock appeared to know every sendaro, every trail. He moved us slow and quiet, and he moved us all day.

Late that evening we arrived at Rancho las Rucias, near the present city of Edinburg. Like a lot of other places hereabouts, this had once been the hacienda of a wealthy Spaniard. But it now showed the wear and tear of the rowdy border life. It was only about ten miles back from the Rio Grande and seemed to belong to anybody who was man enough to hold it.

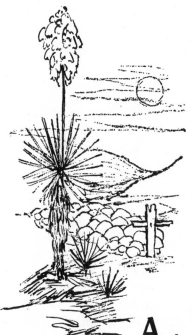

A Near Miss

At the time we got based at Rancho las Rucias business was brisk in cattle thieving. The spring rush was on. The days had been fairly dry in the upper country and the river was lazy and shallow, and stock could be waded across in dozens of places.

It turned out later that Old Rock had sneaked in an agent to the Cortinas headquarters just below Matamoros, a man known as Sergeant George Hall. He had worked with Captain and was a dandy. Old Rock got word that the Cortinas people were shipping by boat more than five thousand beeves every month.

Those men from Congress a few years earlier had reported that Juan Cortinas, the bandit chieftain, had "systematized depredatory war." Cortinas had done this by licensing raiding bandits. Usually he was content with charging them a four-bit crossing fee for using the Rio Grande; then he took his "royal fifth" and paid cash of from two to ten dollars a head, depending on the supply.

For three or four days we worked out of Las Rucias in patrols, without cutting a trail, without sighting a living thing that didn't belong there. Corporal Rudd took three of us on a scout about twenty miles up the river, where we dry camped for the night. The next day we loafed back to Las Rucias, taking a route a few miles inland. Still nothing happened. The patrols were scouting down the river and back toward Los Indios.

Lieutenant Robinson told us it would be all right to limber up our pistols—do a little target practice, something we hadn't yet done. I blazed me a six-inch target off a mesquite, and did some fancy unlimbering.

Being the kid of the outfit, I hadn't been much noticed, but now I had most of the outfit watching—including Captain McNelly. I hadn't bargained for this, but I went at it. I first came in galloping and blazing. I emptied my pistol and hadn't even barked the tree. I reloaded the chamber and came in again at a gallop. I did get a little bark this time.

I dismounted and advanced afoot, blazing away. I did a little better, but was nervous. I wondered what Captain was thinking. I didn't have long to wonder.

I went over to the supply wagon and asked Dad Smith for some more shells. Captain came up behind me. He spoke loud enough for all to hear.

"Sell him some," Captain ordered. "Two bits a round."

"Is his credit good?" Dad asked Captain.

"No. Cash."

This cut me down aplenty. This was the first bawling out

that Captain had given any man in the outfit. And they were all looking and listening.

I must have sort of puddled up. I flipped the cylinder back in my pistol and holstered it, and kept looking at the ground. But I reckon Captain recollected that once when he was a kid my age he joined up with a man's outfit. Maybe he learned the hard way, like I was doing.

"George," he said—he didn't call me son, for the first time —"the state will buy you all the shells you need. But don't waste any more. Practice. You sure need it. But practice— don't put on a show." He turned to Dad Smith and ordered, "Reload him."

I loaded my belt and cylinder, holstered my pistol, stood back not more than five paces from my target, and drew— mighty clumsy. I holstered again and drew slow. I wasn't nervous any more, even with all them watching me. The third time I lifted my pistol I thumbed down the hammer as it came up, in a smooth way. I centered my target with my first shot, naturally. No one could miss at five paces. Then I stepped back five more paces and repeated, lifting my pistol three times before I let the hammer drop.

Captain was watching me and nodded with a little smile as he turned and walked away.

Like most other farm boys of that time, I had handled both pistols and rifles since I was in knee britches. But right now was the first time I came to realize that a pistol wasn't something to show off with, and that when you aimed to use it you needed a clear head and a steady hand.

We mostly fiddled around camp that day. There wasn't any joshing or horseplay, and not much talk. The older hands seemed to be expecting things to pop, and I caught the fever.

Old Rock and Captain huddled quite a bit. But Captain didn't call any of his officers into the talks. They didn't

know any more about what was going on than did the
greenest hand. And they never did. Later on they told me
they never knew three minutes in advance what Captain
had in mind.

The only tip-off we had was that Dad Smith fed us only
hardtack and coffee for supper. That came to be our warning that things was about to stir. Captain believed a man
could fight longer and better on an empty stomach. He had
no use for either a man or horse that couldn't make it thirty-
six hours without rations.

I was tossing my head around on my saddle trying to get
to sleep, well up in the shank of the evening, when I heard
a rider coming in from the north. Our guard was bringing
him in—and took him straight to Captain's tent, where he
reported to Old Rock.

We were all awake when the guard came down the line,
tapped fifteen of us on the shoulder, and told us Captain
said to get ready to ride. Old Rock led off to the north, and
we lined out behind him with Lieutenant Robinson in
charge.

Old Rock would ride you right down to a nubbin. He
always had three, or maybe four, horses portioned to him
in the remuda. He could get more distance out of a horse
than even a Mexican vaquero. He led off in a lope, with us
strung out behind in single file. He took us through soggy
lagunas, up slopes, and across open spaces, always in either
a hard jog or a lope.

Once in a while he hit the brush for a short cut—and he
hit it ducking and riding the side of his horse, nearly losing
some of us. This was all mighty new to me; and even some
of the older hands weren't doing too good in the pale light
of a waning moon.

A couple of hours out, Rock pulled up on a ground swell

and halted the column for a breather and to tighten our cinches. Corporal Rudd hardly ever complained, but he remarked, sort of low, "That man Rock acts loco."

Rock piloted us pretty close along the meanders of the Rio Grande and sometimes we could see the lazy waters shimmering in the moonlight. When day broke, we saw that the river was covered with a silvery ground fog. Rock pulled up at the edge of a sizable sendaro and took his bearings. He got some land signs and caucused with Lieutenant Robinson. He sent Sergeant Armstrong back to the column, and we fanned out in skirmish formation.

"If shooting starts," Sergeant Armstrong ordered, "stop in your tracks and wait for orders. Don't advance. Don't shoot till ordered."

And we began moving behind Rock again. We fanned out, moving slow. The sun was well up when Old Rock moved into the edge of a new-cut trail and halted, shaking his sandy head and cursing, it appeared.

The river fog had burned away, and as we came up we could see, on the other bank, the last of the stolen herd shaking the Rio Grande water from their bellies. Half a dozen drovers were chousing them up the sandy slope.

We had missed by less than an hour. But we had missed.

They had moved that herd almost fifteen miles during the night, as Rock figured. His spy had picked them up about twenty-five miles inland. They had crossed them just above La Bolsa ("The Pocket"), where the river flattened out and was fordable most of the time. It was something like thirty miles or so up from Las Rucias.

Rock guessed they had crossed around three hundred head of beeves and judged there were at least fifty drovers. "Maybe more," he said. "They got more men than old man Carter had oats."

As the outfit moved up into plain sight one of the raiders took off his hat, bowed low in his saddle, and blew us a kiss. Another one thumbed his nose at us and fired his pistol our way once.

Why didn't we get orders to unlimber our Sharps and pick off one or so? Our Sharps would carry across. But the law said no. Firing across from the Texas bank or crossing the river after bandits was against the law, an act of war.

They had driven hard all night and made the river, and had won again. That was now an old story.

Our horses were gaunted. Lieutenant Robinson had us unsaddle so they could stretch and roll and nibble awhile. Then we started back to Las Rucias, drifting easy and slow.

Lieutenant Robinson was not too chipper. He talked some to Rock, but mostly he rode by himself. He dreaded that chewing out from Captain. I was also doing some thinking. Just what in the hell would we have done if we'd been an hour earlier?

There were fifteen of us, and Old Rock said there was not less than fifty of them. All sorts of things ran through my mind, and I reckon all the others were thinking along the same lines.

First of course, we had Sharps carbines that outranged any other shooting equipment. But would that have made up for the difference? One thing for sure—we'd never know.

We missed a fight. We missed breaking up a raid.

We used at least twice as much time getting back as we did coming out from Las Rucias. We sort of straggled and dribbled. Night had fallen when we arrived back.

Captain, old Casoose and one or two other officers were huddled at Captain's tent when Lieutenant Robinson reported.

"We missed," he said. "They were across—"

Captain got up and cut it short. "That's fine," he said with a sneering grin. "That's fine. We're doing as well as the others."

Other patrols had been down the river nearly to Brownsville and had come up with nothing. Which all proved that the Cortinas crowd had the outfit well scouted.

Sending patrols out twenty-five miles each way wouldn't stop anything. The best Captain could wish for would be to find out what had been going on. This wouldn't stop it. And he knew it.

But he wasn't wound up about it. For two days most of us loafed around the camp, taking it easy—all except Casoose and Old Rock. They were gone all the time.

On the third day Casoose rode in about noon, his mount lathered and gaunted. He had made a long and hard ride. He reported to Captain. Right away we were ordered to get ready to move out. Casoose got a fresh mount from the remuda, and he and Rock led out, with fourteen Rangers and Captain McNelly lined in single file.

They headed us back toward Los Indios.

Corporal Rudd told us, as we saddled, "Pull your cinches tight now. There'll be no breathing stops." It meant a forced ride.

For a couple of hours or so we moved fast, in a lope. Old Rock was, as usual, pouring on the leather and crowding his horse. Then he and Casoose waited and caucused with Captain, and the column halted.

Captain sent Maben and Rector on one advance patrol to the left, and Casoose and Parrott on one to the right. The outfit then moved slower and readied.

About sundown, Maben and Rector brought in a captive. He was straddling one of those Dick Heye saddles, and Maben explained, "We thought he might have some talk. That's the reason we brought him in with the saddle."

He was an American. Said he was a gambler and had won

the horse and saddle in a poker game over at Neale's ranch a day or so back. He knew nothing about stock thieves. Just a gambler.

Casoose told Captain, "Maybe he talk for me."

Captain nodded, and Casoose was on him like a panther. He slapped his pistol alongside his head, and when the man went down Casoose lashed his hands behind him with a pigging string, fixed a slip noose around his neck, and dragged him like a log twenty or twenty-five paces to a cottonwood. In no time at all he had him dangling from a limb, fighting for air. But he drew his chin in tight and kept his wind pipe open. He made no sign he would talk.

Ranger Adams said, "Out in California we sometimes churned it out of them, like this—." He lifted the feller a foot or so and let him drop. He did this three or four times; then the man signaled he would talk.

When he got air and could speak, he said he was scouting ahead for a party of men that had raided almost up to La Parra.

"How many raiders?" Captain asked.

The feller said about fifty.

"How many beeves?"

Maybe three hundred, he said.

The raiders were coming back between the Taylor trail and Laguna Madre, hugging the coast closer than they ever did before. If they followed through on that route they would cross the Arroyo Colorado early in the night, at a point a little below the present city of Harlingen, skirt the east edge of Palo Alto prairie, and make the river crossing in eight or ten hours.

That was the way Rock, Casoose and the Captain figured, if this prisoner had talked straight. And it was reasonable to think he had. He was bad shook up and wilted.

Years later I saw a report General Ord had made to

Washington explaining the McNelly success with these rascals. General Ord said:

Captain McNelly had a big advantage over the U. S. troops . mainly because he employed means of getting information from prisoners that was denied the military. His prisoners would talk. Ours wouldn't.

Captain turned the prisoner over to Casoose, and the old man led him out of camp, his hands still lashed behind him. I reckoned Old Casoose had him a prisoner camp off to himself. We didn't have any prisoners. When I found out later it just about turned my stomach.

Every one of us little McNellys knew exactly what we were to do now, and we were saddled and ready to ride. But we learned that only Captain himself knew what he had in mind.

He put us in dry camp for the night, with only the usual patrols out in three-hour shifts. We were to find out he had his reasons—good reasons. While we slept the raiders moved down the coast by the light of a half-moon.

The Fight at Palo Alto

Captain had his plans, all right. He was only waiting for daylight. And when he had settled on a plan and only needed to wait he was almost human. He was calm and easy. From where the raiders were reported to be by the prisoner they had about twenty-five miles to go to the river. Captain pretty well knew how long it took to move a herd that distance.

Well before daylight we were in the saddle and moving east toward the Laguna in a skirmish formation, behind Rock and two advance patrols. Even our saddlebags were weighted with shells, including fifty rounds of those heavy Sharps. You could smell a fight in that salt air.

Excepting the salt flats, this was hardpan country,

brushed mostly with salt cedars, some marsh grass, and scrub-oak motts.

We moved slow for quite a spell toward the Laguna to the east. Then Rock, well in the lead, cut the trail of the stolen herd. The sun was just high enough to burn off most of the ground fog. The trail was only a few hours old at the most, but could have hardly been picked up except in daylight.

He cut it at what I judge now to have been the upperline of the Rincon pasture of old man Neale's ranch. Rock raised up in his saddle, and we could see him circle his hand and drop it, pointing south towards the river, probably fifteen or so miles on.

Rock headed down the trail in a long lope, with Captain leading us in a double column less than half a mile behind. For maybe two miles Rock jogged down that trail, now easy to follow. Then he came out on a pretty fair ground swell, reined up, circled his hand high, and dropped it twice.

He had sighted the gang.

Years later I got a copy of the report Captain made to Austin on the Palo Alto scrap, which this was to be known as, and this was the way it looked to him:

It was about seven o'clock in the morning. We sighted them about eight miles distant, driving hard toward Palo Alto prairie. They discovered my command about the same time and began crowding their herd to the limit. They drove about three more miles and, finding we were closing in on them, they drove the herd onto a little island in the salt marsh, and took their stand in a fringe of brush on the far side of the resaca.

They waited for us about a half hour. They were forted and sheltered and ready for engagement. They fought desperately, every one firing his pistol so long as he could raise up, even when mortally wounded.

To us Rangers it was more like this: Captain galloped up alongside Rock, reined in, lifted out his spy glasses, and for quite a spell he scouted out the scene. The sun had burned off all the ground fog, and we could see with the naked eye the mounted men and the stock. The country was open hardpan, except for a few clumps of dagger and some salt cedar and marsh grass.

Captain dropped his glasses back in his saddle pocket, lifted his pistol, broke out the cylinder, flicked it back, tested the trigger works, and holstered it.

He kneed Segal around so that he was headed for the bandits, gave one look back to see if we were in place, then buried his rowels in the sides of that big bay.

Segal took off like a turpentined cat. Captain must have known better than to gig a blooded horse; he came mighty near losing his saddle. Segal cleared a rod or better that first leap, and his hooves flung hardpan cakes fifty feet high. We took in behind, but he pulled away from us like our horses were hobbled.

He had got the bit in his teeth and had gone cold jawed. He was plumb out of control. Sometimes he was out of our sight. But when he showed up again he was still headed straight for the target.

Captain said the bandits waited half an hour. It must have been longer than that. Even Segal couldn't have covered the distance in that time. He was slowed to a jog when Captain hove up at the edge of the resaca, five hundred or so yards from the bandits shelter.

He circled Segal to a walk, and when we got bunched around him he give us a pep talk. "Boys," he said, "across this resaca are some outlaws that claim they're bigger than the law—bigger than Washington law, bigger than Texas law. Right now we'll find out if they're right or if they're wrong. This won't be a standoff or a dogfall. We'll either win completely, or we'll lose completely.

"Those cutthroats have plundered and raided and murdered at will. They've mistreated our women and carried off some in slavery.

"You will follow me in a skirmish line spaced at five-pace intervals. Don't fire a shot until I do. Don't shoot either to your right or left. Shoot only at the target directly in front."

While we were huddling they sent across a few shots, but they all fell short and only splashed the thin resaca water. A sizable bunch was still mounted and holding the herd off to our left on that little island. Some others were mounted and drifting around in the rear. They were well forted for a standoff fight till they could get more men from across the river and move the herd.

They hardly expected Captain to break out of that huddle the way he did. He headed Segal their way and jogged him up a little. He splashed in the hock-deep resaca, and we were right behind him in skirmish line. They must have panicked for a spell. We didn't draw much fire till the line was halfway across. Then it started getting heavy.

They had taken good shelter and waited more than half an hour. They were set to swap a few shots across that quarter-mile-wide resaca. But they weren't forted for a charge.

Some of them broke for their horses and turned tail across the prairie. The ones that didn't break were doing some mighty wild shooting. When Captain brought us into pistol range they still were shooting wild, shooting low.

And Captain wasn't shooting at all. He was putting the rowels to Segal, getting in closer. That must have spooked them. It sure spooked me.

I was third man down from Corporal Rudd when his

horse went down and he jumped clear, barely getting his carbine loose. Several of the horses were raring and twisting. They had taken some hits. The line was now less than a hundred paces from the brush. More of the bandits were boarding their horses and scampering away. But plenty of them were staying.

Captain kept closing in, holding his fire. Up till right now I hadn't panicked. But my horse fell to his knees, and when I couldn't bring him up I grabbed my carbine and jumped clear. Then I prayed, and meant it. Every bone in me said turn back. I couldn't go another foot closer. I was paralyzed. It hadn't hit me so strong as long as I had a horse under me. But now, afoot in that muddy resaca, I couldn't move. So I prayed for the Good Lord to not let me turn back.

Then at not more than thirty paces Captain got a target and opened fire with his pistol. The Good Lord had answered my prayer. When I came to my senses I was still facing that brush line and splashing in closer, my Sharps cocked and at firing level.

Three or four steps closer, and I had me a target. He came up from the shelter of a clump of scrub salt cedar. His hat showed first, and he was in my target area—right smack dab in front. He came up to get away; he was turned for a horse in the rear. Under that big fancy beaver hat I saw a white scar down the right cheek, from the hairline to the chin. I got that scar in my sight and dropped the hammer. Both hat and head seemed to explode.

I had made my first shot in combat and I hit my target. I had brought down the prize—that scar-faced dude who had quirted down Martha Noakes. Right then I quit being a scared country boy. I was a man. A Ranger. A little McNelly.

Captain and all hands were dismounted and in the brush,

afoot. Firing was steady all along the line. Segal, I noticed, was performing like a real champ. He stood, ground hitched, right where Captain had dropped his reins. The other horses were milling some. Most of them had flesh wounds.

The brush line was not more than twenty paces deep— just up the slope from the resaca edge to the prairie. As our hands started mopping up, some of the bandits still on their feet were breaking for their mounts. But they had waited too long.

Two of them had mounted one horse and were spurring away when Lieutenant Wright got in a good carbine shot. One rolled from behind the saddle; the other tumbled twenty paces farther on.

Lieutenant Wright grinned wide. "Dadblame if I didn't get dubs," he said. "Captain only ordered us to get one with each shot. Reckon he'll charge me for that?"

Captain had his area quieted, except for one outlaw who was well hidden behind a clump of marsh grass. He wasn't firing any more, but he wasn't dead. Ten paces away, Captain called out loud, "My pistol's empty. Bring me some more shells."

It worked. The outlaw broke cover, a knife flashing. He opened his mouth in a wide grin as he came charging. And Captain got him right in his big mouth.

Captain had mounted, and he rode out on the hard ground. Lieutenant Wright was close to the first one he had shot from behind the saddle. He motioned Captain.

"He's asking for a chaplain," Wright said. "He must be a war veteran. He wants a chaplain before he goes out."

The old outlaw had taken that Sharps right below the rib cage and was bad torn up and going out fast.

Captain asked no questions. He dismounted, holstered his pistol, and took a testament from his jacket pocket. He came up to the dying outlaw, not as the Captain of a Texas Ranger outfit but as a Virginia minister. He was bent over reading the Scripture to him when the man went out.

Down on our right flank, Rangers Adams and Smith moved in afoot, mopping up. One outlaw broke and was mounting when Smith got in a pistol shot and brought him down. He was slashing the grass and floundering when Smith came up too close. The outlaw rolled over, got one shot into Smith, and killed the Ranger in his tracks.

In the last part of Captain's report to Austin he wrote:

I have never seen men fight with such desperation. Many of them, after being shot from their horses and severely wounded three or four times, would rise on their elbows and empty their pistols at us with their dying breath. After they broke cover it was a succession of fights, man to man, for five or six miles across the prairie. . . .

I got in the running fight, mounted on an outlaw's horse. He was a good one. He had a Running W burned on his left hip, and any animal with that brand was good. That was Captain King's brand.

We didn't have too good shooting out in the open. What was left of the bandits had a jump on us, and they were fogging it for the river. I got only one rifle shot, a long one, and made a clean miss. Some of the others were having better luck.

I stayed in sight of Corporal Rudd. When there was nothing left to shoot at he waved in his three men and said Lieutenant Robinson had called the fight off. It was now well along towards high noon, about four hours since Captain had first sighted the bandits. It had been a good morning's work. One that went down in the history books.

Captain had pulled away some time earlier and ordered all hands be gathered in and put in dry camp at the edge of

Brownsville. He took Lieutenant Wright, Sergeant Armstrong, and Sergeant Orrill with him and rode directly to the Miller Hotel in Brownsville.

There he introduced himself. "My name's McNelly," he said. "Lee McNelly. I want to rent two rooms. Two big downstairs rooms for a headquarters."

"What sort of headquarters?" Miller asked.

"Ranger headquarters. We're Texas Rangers."

"Shore 'nuf?" Miller replied. "We heard some Rangers were having a fight out at Palo Alto this morning. Was that you all?"

"That was us."

"Anybody get hurt?"

"Yes. I want to sign for two rooms. The state will pay you."

"You say your name's McNelly? Would that be Captain McNelly?"

"That's right."

"Well, why in the hell didn't you say so? You ain't on the dodge, are you?" Then he added, "I don't want my place shot up if they come after you—understand?"

Captain's blood was still hot and he was fractious. He bit into a cigar and began pacing.

"You've got rooms to rent," he said. "I've rented these two front ones. We're moving in."

It turned out that Luis Saldana, a deputy sheriff, had been rounded up yesterday by two of our boys and brought to camp. When Captain came in some time later he let the deputy go, after looking over his papers. This morning Sheriff Browne had taken a posse of some ten men out to Palo Alto, but had come back without us seeing him.

Down through the years there has been wild talk about hard feelings between Sheriff Browne and Captain McNelly. But I think this is all there was to it. Sheriff Browne was maybe riled because we had held one of his deputies. But our boys were under orders to bring anybody to camp.

Captain did go around Sheriff Browne right now. He ordered Lieutenant Wright to fetch the brand inspector and the U. S. marshal. Usually he would have reported to the sheriff. That was the custom governing Rangers. When they operated in a county they reported to the sheriff.

When the brand inspector, John J. Smith, came in Captain got right to the point. "We captured a drove of cattle on Palo Alto prairie this morning," he said. "I want you to take possession of them, dispose of them according to law. Find the brand owners if you can. Sell the rest as directed by law. I want your written report."

To Marshal Joe O'Shaughnessy he gave the same orders. "My boys had a fight at Palo Alto this morning. I want you to take charge of the plunder and turn it over to the court for disposition. You'll need a wagon for that. I want you to bring the bodies in to me for identification. You'll need an army ambulance for that."

"How many bodies, Captain?"

"I don't know. There are several. Gather them up."

Captain was as cool as a blue norther. Fact is, he appeared in good spirits. He had come through another good hard fight, and fighting seemed to be his business. He was on top and giving orders and they were being obeyed.

He next ordered Lieutenant Wright to rush orders up to Las Rucias and bring all the hands to Brownsville. He told Wright to set up camp at the edge of town and to hold all hands at the ready. He appeared to think the fighting wasn't over.

Major Anderson loaned a light wagon and ambulance to the marshal; then he came to the Miller Hotel and met Captain. The Major said he expected the Cortinas men to come across in force if Palo Alto checked out as bad as he'd heard in first reports. Some years before, when some of Cortinas' men had come off bad with Texas law, Cortinas had come acro₅s the river, captured and looted Brownsville, captured and plundered Fort Brown.

Cortinas wasn't a common border outlaw. I believe he was the third generation of a Spanish family that had owned the Espiritu Santo grant of 260,000 acres, including the present city of Brownsville. He had been governor of Tamaulipas and had kinfolks and friends on both sides of the river. And plenty of licensed riders.

"I've got half a company of infantry," Major Anderson told Captain. "We can fight on the Texas bank to throw back an invasion. You make the plans and give us the orders. We'll bury your dead Rangers with military honors, and we'll patch up your wounded at our infirmary."

As the day wore on the fever in Brownsville went higher. All sorts of reports and wild rumors were going the rounds. The worst one was that some well-known Brownsville stock traders had bought a herd of cattle and were bringing them down peacefullike when jumped by the Rangers, that even after the fight opened they tried to surrender but were slaughtered while waving the white flag.

Whether or not all this wild talk got to Captain, I don't know. He ordered Corporal Rudd to bring in four of his hands, and I was one of them. Our camp had been pitched out at the edge of town, right near Fort Brown.

None of our men had anything worse than flesh wounds. Not a bone or a holler had been damaged. The doc at the fort fixed them all in no time. We had only one dead—Sonny Smith. Adams brought him in and carried him to the fort chapel.

At about an hour by sun, Marshal O'Shaughnessy got back, with three soldiers on the ambulance that was piled high with saddles and gear.

"We got fourteen saddles and quite a passel of firearms," he said to Captain, pointing to the wagon.

"Ask the court to dispose of them," Captain ordered.

Pointing to the ambulance, the Marshal said, "We gathered up sixteen bodies. Mostly up around the resaca and the edge of the prairie, where the main fight took place. We scoured around the prairie some, but only found three there."

Captain came outside and pointed to a spot on the plaza near where the water fountain now stands. "Stack the bodies up over there," he ordered. "Out in the open."

And the soldiers stacked those outlaw bodies up like cordwood, over by the fountain.

This was Captain's answer to the big mouths and wild talkers. He figured they had threatened a fight. He wanted to get it over with. He ordered Sergeant Armstrong to post an eight-man guard around the plaza to arrest any person coming up to identify the bodies, and to bring him in to headquarters at the Miller Hotel.

When dark had settled Captain got with Major Anderson. They posted a soldier guard on the river and tied up the ferry for the night. No one was to cross from either side.

Captain was on top of the situation, and as cool as the back of a well-digger's lap.

The Brownsville air that night of June 12, 1875, was heavy with fight. The Cortinistas had taken their worst licking in their history, and a licking is something a bandit leader can't take without striking back, quick.

But not a one of us McNellys was jittery. We had us a boss who we now knew wouldn't let us go into a fight we couldn't win. Because we were still shorthanded they didn't change our guard all night. But it didn't seem too long. A good half-moon lighted up the plaza till well after midnight, I'd judge. And all we had to do was watch that stack of dead bandits. Nobody came to try and get one, and none of the dead bandits tried to leave. It was an easy patrol.

They said that after Captain checked his patrols and river guards he went back to the Miller Hotel, put a cot in one of the rooms, and got three or four hours sound sleep. He did business that way.

The rest of the company from Las Rucias got into the Brownsville camp a little after sunup. They had made a hard ride and didn't know much, except it had been a hell of a fight at Palo Alto and that another one was in the making.

Captain got a soldier detail to relieve us on patrol and took us all out to our camp. He went to Fort Brown and used the military telegraph to report the fight to Austin. He then came to our camp, right near, and ordered a roll call. Then he gave us some instructions. "Don't any of you," he said, "go into Brownsville except when ordered. Stay close to camp, ready for orders. We might have to move fast on short notice."

One of the hands from Las Rucias said, "Captain, you figuring on ordering us across the river?"

Captain didn't answer him direct. Instead he walked down to him and asked, "You want your discharge? Is that what you're driving at?"

"I ain't going to cross the river to fight," he half-whined.

"Fall out of ranks and wait at my tent for your discharge," Captain said. He stepped back and asked, "Anybody else want to quit now?"

There were more. Six, all told.

With a cold, sneering smile he scribbled out their discharges, giving as reason, "Not needed."

"Our pay ought to come down in a day or so," he told them.

"Can we stay in camp till it comes?" one asked.

"If the others will let you," he replied.

Captain knew we wouldn't. The men knew we wouldn't.

There wasn't a one of them that had been at Palo Alto. They had a month's wages due and hadn't fired a shot in combat.

As soon as they had checked in their state property to the sergeant they were on their own. Out of it they each had a damn sight better horse than the one they had brought in.

Old W6 Wright up at Banquette knew a good bet. So did Captain. Both knew there would be some cutbacks, some fallouts. My throat sort of dried up when I remembered how close I had come to turning back. Again I thanked the Good Lord for not letting me do that.

A messenger came down from Fort Brown and reported to Captain with a stiff military salute. That's the way they rated Captain. Then the word was passed that we would go to the fort for breakfast. Those were the best words I had heard for heaven knows how long.

I didn't remember when I had eaten last. It seemed to have been back in Georgia. I was empty down to the soles of my boots. It was only a short piece to the fort and I was halfway there before that soldier got through his saluting.

My nose took me direct to the mess hall. It was a long hall, and inside at the far end a smiling old Negro cook was batching up flapjacks and frying long strips of good streaked side meat.

Captain had said we'd eat breakfast at the fort, and I wasn't waiting for further orders. They had butter and molasses, blackstrap molasses. And coffee. Barrels of it.

As I loaded up, that old cook grinned wide and said, "I sho' likes to see a hungry boy eat."

Captain and Major Anderson caucused and agreed they'd bury our boy this morning. In those days burying couldn't wait too long in hot weather.

Then the Major ordered up a two-seated carryall, and Captain went back to the Miller Hotel, taking along Sergeant Orrill, Corporal Rudd, Maben, and me.

He moved fast to get rid of the bodies stacked on the plaza. He sent for Marshal O'Shaughnessy and told him to take off the military patrol and send them back to the fort. He said to turn the bodies over to Sheriff Browne.

"You all identify all you can," he ordered, "and let me have your report."

We and the soldiers gave Ranger Sonny Smith the biggest burial Brownsville had seen in many a day. His box, lying in the open bed of a light wagon, was covered with a flag. Captain headed a column of Rangers, afoot, and a half-dozen or so squads of soldiers come next. We circled the streets of Brownsville. Then as we headed for the military graveyard the Rangers fell out and turned back. Smith was buried with full military honors.

They made a big show of it, I reckon, to let everyone know that Fort Brown was solid behind Captain McNelly. It probably saved some trouble, because the people of Brownsville were still sullen from listening to all the talk going around.

A Time for Loafing

After Marshal O'Shaughnessy had sorted out the wagonload of plunder he gathered up at Palo Alto, his report to Captain showed he had recovered from the scene and off the bodies of the dead bandits a total of twenty-two pistols, twelve rifles, and fourteen saddles.

"Nine of the saddles," he said, "look to be almost brand new. They are dandies. Garnished with two-inch silver conchos, foot-long tapideros. The first ones I've seen. Came from Dick Heye saddlery at Santone."

Captain perked up and said, "Let's have a look at them. Sounds like they're part of the plunder taken up at Nuecestown in a raid last March."

They were. No mistaking them.

Captain was mighty pleased. "Have the judge send them back to Nuecestown," he said firmly. "They're part of the loot from that raid."

They weren't ordinary saddles, and the bandits who had been riding them weren't ordinary mill-run bandits. They were *jefes*. Top hands in the Cortinas set up.

Five of the dead bandits had been identified as citizens of Brownsville—Cortinas had men and kinfolks on both sides of the river. Rustling stock was no disgrace in his books. He called the stock "grandma's cattle," and he could win if you'd argue the finer points.

When the Mexican state of Texas won independence the boundary between Texas and Tamaulipas was the Nueces River. General Houston set the boundary at the Rio Grande when Texas was annexed, and General Taylor made it stick. At least on the maps. But Cortinas did a lot to unstick it.

It wasn't too surprising that some names which stood in Brownsville for respected people were found to be on the list of those trafficking in rustled stock. But right now it was plumb awkward they were caught in Palo Alto. It made a lot of good folks hate Captain McNelly. He didn't fight according to the rules. A lot of false rumors sprang up now.

Among other things some people said that some of them at Palo Alto were trying to surrender when shot down. Maybe so. I didn't see any white flags.

But what ran fever the highest was Captain stacking the dead on the plaza overnight, with a guard. Of course, Captain was trying to bait a raid from across the river. I doubt if he knew any of the dead were Brownsville people whose kinfolks wanted to claim them.

Wild talk that the dead men had been on a stock-buying trip in the upper country didn't stand up much when the brand inspector made his report. He had brought

in 240 beeves, and right away he located some brand owners. They all said they had lost their stock to bandits who
came in force, killing herdsmen and vaqueros who stood in
their way. This was the same old story—up till the raiders
made their stand at Palo Alto. The military said that till
then making a stand and then surrendering was a regular
trick, when the military was in the picture. All the soldiers
could do was accept the surrender, turn them over to the
courts, and see the raiders make bond and be back in business in a day or so.

As for proving they had raided any stock—you couldn't
even prove any stock was in their charge. A herd of stock
being around in their area meant nothing; stock was everywhere, as this was back in the days before barbed wire.

Captain began staying inside the rooms more and more
every day. He was bothered with a bad cough. Most of
the orders for the hands now came down through his officers, mainly Lieutenant Robinson. They kept me around
quite a bit of the time doing chores and running errands.
But I never got inside much and sometimes didn't see Captain all day long. When I did, he sure looked peaked. But
he didn't appear to get any skinnier—he was skinny to
begin with.

He never did get up and eat in the dining room with the
others, but instead sort of snacked in his room. Of course,
the word had already got around that Captain was a consumptive, and in those days nobody wanted to eat in the
same room with a consumptive. No hotel wanted to rent
one a room.

About the only people who got past Robinson to see the
Captain were Old Rock, and Charley Stillman, and a medi-
cal man from the fort. Stillman had a store and a bank, and

he threw in with Captain from the start. He cashed our state scrip without deducting, and went out of his way to help us. He fixed it up so Captain could get a better room off to himself at the Brown Hotel, and the medic began sending in goat milk twice a day.

Out at our camp the hands killed time and waited orders. The military gave us a box of lye soap and the Major loaned us a set of horse clippers. We shingled each other up, and bathed and washed our clothes down at the river.

We all had walking-around money on us now, and time on our hands. That usually spells trouble. Add a little mescal and a señorita or two—well, that mescal is powerful, and the little saddle-colored señoritas had a way about them.

But orders came down through Lieutenant Robinson that we had to leave our pistols in camp when we went to town. They all told him, hell, they'd rather leave their britches. The next day he said we could go to town carrying our pistols only when not more than three of us went with our corporal, and that we were not to lift a pistol unless signaled by the corporal. We were not at any time to enter a cantina, and we were to be back in camp before dark.

That went on for several days. We jawed about it, but we all knew the order made sense—like all of Captain's orders. A good many folks still had hard feelings toward us, and that always makes some of the show-off killers want to notch their pistol butts again.

The next time Corporal Rudd took us to town we were browsing through Charley Stillman's store, jingling our money and wishing. My Georgia farm duds sure weren't going to get me anywhere in Texas high society. I began noticing them more all the time. My old boots were cracked, and some hair still showed on them. My hat was a floppy, thin piece of felt to begin with.

I was fingering one of Stillman's best hats. It was a dandy piece of heavy felt. I creased it and tried it on. It just fit. I looked inside at the price and was laying it down when Stillman himself came up, smiling, and said,

"Keep it on if you want it, son."

Corporal Rudd said just one word. "No."

It was marked more than a month's wages.

"Half that price," Mr. Stillman said.

Corporal Rudd said three words this time. "No. Come on."

Outside I took off my old hat and began whimpering. "Shucks, Corporal—"

"You recollect," he said, "Captain ordered us not to take even a melon or roasting ear without paying for it. That goes for hats and boots. You think the man offered you a hat on account of you're a cotton-chopping country boy from Georgia?"

"No. I reckon it's because he likes Captain McNelly, and I'm working for Captain."

But I might as well have spent my month's wages and bought that hat. Back in camp, Boyd had a horse blanket spread down under a big cottonwood and was dealing stud. I sat in, and that was where my month's wages went—for the time being. I got them back later.

Parrott, the man who took pictures with the circus, had a blanket spread down too and was shuffling three walnut shells, the best being to pick the shell that hid a bean. Jim Wofford, who had been losing right along, saw something suspicious. Fighting words passed, and both men came to their knees, their pistols clearing leather. But Sergeant Orrill had read the weather signs and when the storm was about to strike he stepped between them. Then he ordered no more gambling in camp.

Most of us by this time were plenty tired of killing time

around camp. We wondered if Captain was too sick to go on. If he was, what would be done with us?

Captain was sick and puny all right, but his brain wasn't. He had his plans. All we had to do was wait and he'd tell us about them, with maybe five minutes warning.

Rudd was picked for the Captain's detail the next day, and he took me in again. They had moved the Captain, this time to a fair-sized adobe house in a big cottonwood grove. Captain was lying out in the open under a big tree, on a field cot.

A woman was puttering around the cookstove and a boy was wrestling with a Mexican burro. They were the Captain's wife and son. Lieutenant Robinson made us all acquainted. The lady was mighty nice. The boy pooched out his jaws and let go a sort of horse laugh. His name was Rebel, and it fit him.

That army medic had sent for Mrs. McNelly—Carrie—without saying anything to Captain. He figured the Captain must have some good grub and plenty of rest. That was all they knew to do for consumption in those days.

Lieutenant Robinson gave me a paper and told me to take it to Sheriff Browne. I held it in my hand and walked to the courthouse. When I walked in the Sheriff's room two or three men were talking but they all quit at once.

"I got a paper for Sheriff Browne," I said.

A heavy-set, square-bodied man reached out his hand and said, "I'm the sheriff. What is that? Who's it from?"

"Captain McNelly," I said.

He sized me up as he unfolded the paper and asked, "Are you one of his men?"

"Yes, sir," I replied.

"Where you from?"

"Georgia."

"How old are you?"

I didn't much like all this, so I said, "Old enough."

"Have you," he asked, "got one of the books—one of those books full of names?"

"Yes, sir."

"Could I borrow it?"

"No, sir."

"Could I look at it?"

"No, sir."

"Uh huh. A feisty, sassy kid. Does this Captain of yours know most of that list is several years old? That lots of those people have married, settled down? Ranchers. Some been elected to public office. Some of our best citizens. Does your Captain know that?"

"The Captain's the man to answer that," I said.

He fumbled around among some papers and took out one that he handed me and said," This is what he sent you for. The list of who we buried. I—"

I got the paper and said, "Much obliged," and left.

When I handed it to Lieutenant Robinson he said, "You take it to the Captain. He wants to see you. But don't say anything about his being sick. You hear?"

Captain was sitting propped up in the bed. It was well-shaded and a sight cooler than away from those trees. He had some color in his cheeks and showed some life.

I handed him the paper and said, "Lieutenant Robinson told me to give this to you."

He unfolded it and scanned it. "It's the list," he said. Then he counted down and declared, "Sixteen. I thought there were more than that."

I began backing away, and he said, "I was in my first shooting skirmish at about your age, George. My captain gave me a little pat on the back and it helped a lot.

"I caught you in the corner of my eye at Palo Alto and you did all right. You came through in good shape. You learn fast. Keep it up, and you'll make a good peace officer."

As he talked I took off my old hat and twisted it around some. Then I blurted out, "I came mighty near not making it, sir."

"Before we opened fire—before the shooting started?"

"Yes, sir. I had to pray hard to keep from turning back."

"That's natural," he half-smiled. "That's human. Only a man's being on the right side lets him hold his fire till he gets his target. Those on the wrong side have to hear shooting, else they panic—as you saw them do at Palo Alto."

I studied a minute and said, "Supposing some of their wild shots hit the target?"

"Fighting," he said, "is a chancy business. Whether man-to-man or in company, both sides have guns, both sides aim to win. Praying makes the difference. A man who's in the right can pray. A man on the wrong side can't. And a peace officer doing his sworn duty is on the right side. He's protected, up till it's his time to go out. That might be from an outlaw bullet, from a stumbling horse, or between bed sheets under a roof. The Scripture says that the day and hour are set the day a man's born."

I glanced back and saw Old Rock waiting. So I left. Every word Captain had said sunk deep in my mind and stayed there—now for more than half a century.

He said I was learning fast and that I ought to make a good hand. Captain McNelly had said that. To me. And gave me some mighty sound rules for winning a gun fight.

Come noon that day I ate my first meal of cabrito—Mexican goat. Miss Carrie—Captain's wife—had a Mexican woman helping and the woman had cooked a ten-pound kid. And a big pan of soda biscuits, with onions and frijoles. I've eaten a million meals of cabrito since, but none ever tasted as good as that first one.

They unjointed the goat and gave Captain the whole

saddle. We watched him eat just about all of it except the bones. They were sure loading him with goat milk and goat meat, and it appeared to be getting some flesh on him.

I walked out with Lieutenant Robinson, patted my belly, and said, "Food like that, and wages too, for loafing. I reckon my wages are still going on, ain't they?"

He smiled some and said, "Yes. You go right ahead and take the money. You'll be earning it now pretty quick."

"You mean the outfit's going to get moving?"

"That's the general idea."

"When?"

"When Captain gives the order."

Robinson followed me out on the gallery and seemed to want to talk some more, which made me feel a little important. "Captain is sick all right," he said. "But he ain't through, like he wants some folks to think. He's had lung trouble a long time, and he has these times when he has to go to bed. But he always gets back on his feet when the time comes.

"Since Palo Alto he's let things simmer—but simmer his way. Since that first bunch quit the outfit they got the word around that lots of others were quitting and that Captain's planning to go back home with his wife as soon as he's able.

"But Captain has used this lull to build his spy system. A bunch of stockmen are letting Old Rock hire outlaws for spies, and Rock and Casoose can guarantee to pay in good gold for spy work that nets any bandits on this side. You can bet Captain will have notice of any raids before they get back across the river. He gets reports every day, starting with George Hall right in the Cortinas headquarters.

"Since his Civil War days in Louisiana Captain has been has been known as a chicken-hawk kind of leader. He dabs down where he ain't expected."

By having this talk with me Lieutenant Robinson had given me a pat on the back too. He figured I could keep my mouth shut.

Except for the two or three men used to run chores for the Captain, we loafed around camp. Some of us took a bath and washed our shirts and socks every day down at the river. It was nothing for two or three of us to make a pasear down through Brownsville in daytime. The folks all seemed to know every one of us, and they weren't too friendly. How they knew us I couldn't figure out. We wore work clothes like all the other menfolks. We carried pistols like all other menfolks. We didn't have badges. But they knew us.

One morning four of us were walking to town when a carriage overhauled us right at the edge of the plaza, and a mighty fetching little señorita had her flunky stop while she got out. The carriage and all she wore looked upper crust. She had a silver tray across her lap. When she uncovered it we saw a pan of dulces that were still hot.

She handed the tray our way, and we all shucked off our hats and reached for one. She smiled friendlylike, offered us another round, and then put the lacy cover back on. I reckon she was on her way to some sort of a sociable cooky nibble, but she was the first one who had treated us like we were anything but varmints.

We figured our luck was changing and we naturally tried to crowd it. We sort of reckoned we'd take a place in Brownsville society. But our first society outing changed our minds. It came on a Saturday night when we heard the music from the Mexican *baile* start from down at the edge of Brownsville. Four or five of us drifted there. It was in a regular *baile* or dance room, with a row of benches down one side for the men and a row down the other side for the women. The little band was going strong when we arrived.

The dancing and music stopped. We were lined up proper on the side for men, but a deputy with a badge and pistol thumbed toward the door and said "Git." Well, we hadn't been invited. No one had asked us to come. So all of us backed toward the door, except Boyd. He knew we had orders to back away from a fight with the natives, but he wasn't in any hurry, and the deputy took his arm and shoved him some.

Boyd was on him like a panther and knocked him down with his fist. Our orders were only not to draw our pistols. A knife flashed in the lamplight and we saw the blade sink in Boyd's heavy duck jacket.

As I said before, Boyd was a knife fighter, the best in our outfit—the best, in fact, I've ever seen. His reach was way longer than the average, and he was a limber as a wet rope. His knife flashed, and you could hear bones crunch. One went down and Boyd began backing away. We went outside, and Boyd followed. He wasn't hurt bad, and we scampered back to camp.

Boyd only had one puncture, under the rib cage on the left side. His duck jacket had caught most of it, and the cut wasn't deep.

Dad Smith, who sort of doubled as our medic, looked at the cut and told Boyd to go up and let the army medic swab it out and sew it up. Boyd said no. Dad said yes, on account of he didn't have any good swab. Boyd said dab it with some tequila and it would grow together. And that's what he did.

Boyd hadn't gone with us when we ate at the fort. He had got a flesh wound at Palo Alto, but he hadn't gone with the others to let the army medics swab that out. He hadn't gone near the army—and wasn't going.

Years later he stopped overnight at a cow camp I was running, and he told me why he shied away from the army.

They wanted him back in California. While trying to stop a breakout from an army stockade, an army officer had been killed with a cypress water bucket. Boyd was in that stockade by the name of Bobo. So they were looking for him in Texas, looking everywhere but in our Ranger outfit. I'm damn sure Captain didn't know this. He'd have handed him over if they'd asked him and identified the man.

Betrayal

The summer slump came to an end one evening when Captain rode into camp on Segal, the same as if he'd been riding in every day. But all hands knew we'd be moving pretty sharp.

We could feel things tightening up in camp. We had beeen loafing so long we had got a mite careless. But with Captain back we handily fell into a tight ready. Lieutenant Wright ordered us in for roll call, the first one for some time. He counted us off, and all were there.

Then Captain paraded before us with a little Frenchy-looking feller no bigger than Captain but a dude and dandy all the way.

"This feller," Captain said businesslike, "is down in The

Book as Pete Marsele. Scratch him. Work with him. He'll
be in and out of camp, and working some patrols. See that
he's not harmed."

Everything about Pete was fancy. He had a diamond in
his shirt and fringes on his doeskin jacket. He was in The
Book as a gambler and a killer, with five lines of black type.
A good many of us didn't trust this Pete, but we figured
Captain knew what he was doing.

Word came down that we were moving camp in the
morning, and we were glad to hear that. We were going
back to work.

Before we moved the next morning Casoose rode in with
a compadre. He caucused with Captain, and Captain called
us into formation and cleared this new man. He was down
in the The Book as Old Blas. Nothing else. Captain told us
to scratch him and see no harm came to him. Captain never
did order him back in The Book, and the old cutthroat
used that clearance for forty years—till Pershing crossed
over and flushed him out and killed him.

Blas was a crafty old butcher. Years later when one of the
Rangers stole Old Blas' girl friend he rigged up a deal
whereby this Ranger killed her by mistake one foggy morning—a neat little trick that was told to the writer O. Henry
who made a story out of it.

One thing we didn't take along when we moved out was
that boy of Captain's. He got to breaking away from the
house and coming out to camp mighty near every day. He
messed with everything, but he liked to play with our pistols
better than most anything else. At first we sort of toadied to
him, on account of his being the Captain's boy. But then
some of the older men decided if he was big enough to play
with a pistol he was big enough to spat.

To keep him pacified some of the hands would empty
their chambers and let the kid practice with an empty gun.

He learned pretty quick how to lay the hammer back and snap it, using both hands.

One day Parrott and Rudd and I got a bar of soap and started to the river. This kid Rebel tried to tag along. Parrott shooed him back once or twice, but he came on; and Rudd caught him and give him a paddling. We thought he had turned back, but he hadn't. Rebel waited until we'd shucked off our clothes and were in the water; then he showed up out of the brush, got himself a loaded pistol, and began banging away at us in the water.

He got off three shots, aiming with both hands, and not missing near far enough before Rudd circled in behind him and disarmed him. Then he really set his little britches on fire.

When Captain came back into action he sent his wife and boy back to Burton on the stagecoach.

We got to Las Rucias by sundown and found it wasn't the same place. The pens had been fixed and were full of horses, of a dozen or more brands. They were grain-fed and slick as butter. There were a dozen or so hands and vaqueros still looking after corrals and traps and feed bins and sheds. The ranchers and stockmen were getting behind Captain with something more than talk.

With thieving active along more than 150 miles of Rio Grande country it might appear that Captain with twenty-nine men couldn't put much of a crimp in it. Well, Captain didn't try till he got his spy system set up. He didn't give a damn for knowing how many got back across. He wanted a spy system that would put him there at the crossing with some men, ahead of the raiders. They were coming across now in little dabs of six or eight, at different crossings, gathering a good herd back inland, then driving like hell for a crossing up around Las Cuevas and Camargo—a hundred miles up the river.

Right after Captain began sending us out on patrols four of us—Parrott, Hardy, Casoose, and I—took cover about fifteen miles up the river, at a spot where Casoose planted us. We were under orders to take alive any little bunches, or at least some of the raiders, so they could be questioned in camp.

Casoose's calculations were right. The moon was full and we saw these two come cantering down the sendaro some time before we stepped from cover, our carbines leveled. They took it like old hands at surrendering. They were well armed and well mounted—one of them straddled a Dick Heye saddle. They were top hands, and a good catch. We disarmed them and turned them over to Casoose.

On the chance they might be advance scouts for a raiding band we pointed toward camp down the river and told Casoose to be on his way. We would wait an hour or so. Maybe another patrol would come looking for these. That would be the regular way.

In a little while we heard some noise from down the river a quarter of a mile or so. Horses stomped; then a man tried to holler. We figured Casoose had hubbed himself some trouble with his prisoners. We pulled away from the sendaro, mounted our horses, and hustled on down to help him.

But he didn't need any help. By the time we got there each bandit had been pulled loose from his head. Bound tight, each had been lashed to a tree by the neck; then Casoose had looped the feet with his rawhide lariat and slapped his horse. That was it.

Old Casoose had put his hat on the ground and was looking up, crossing himself. White foam was dropping off his chin, and his eyes were blazing fire.

I heard tales back in the early days of men going crazy after losing their womenfolks to the Indians—crazy only when they got their hands on an Indian. It was the same thing with Casoose and the bandits. He lived only to kill them. Having lost his wife and daughter to them, he hated those rascals to the day he died.

We didn't watch too long. My stomach started turning flips. We went back up to the sendaro and took cover. But nothing more came our way. We stayed nested up till up in the morning. Then we moved up the river—and cut a fresh trail not more than a few hours old.

It hadn't been a big herd. Around a hundred head, we figured, and just about that many drovers. It had crossed not more than five miles from where we spent the night. A pretty neat maneuver. When the two scouts failed to return, the others turned the cattle some north and made the crossing about daylight. It had cost them two men, but men they had aplenty. Beeves were now worth up to ten dollars a head on the Mexican side. Men were worth nothing.

Fact is, we heard that beeves across the river were now going for as high as twelve dollars. They were scarce, and the Cortinistas had some big contracts.

We turned back toward camp empty-handed. We didn't have any prisoners—at least not any that could talk. We had nested down like mother hens and had let a herd get across nearly in hearing distance. But what would we have done if we'd flushed them? Four of us, without Captain to plan and lead us. We had just missed. And that's all that Captain would need to hear. We had netted a sum total of one Dick Heye saddle.

Back in camp we reported to Sergeant Armstrong, Captain being out on a scout. We took out The Book and began trying to identify the two dead.

"Needn't mind names," Armstrong cut in. "Captain doesn't want them told to him, else he's got to report them to Austin—and this time that's too much writing." Then he pointed to Parrott and said, "You report to Captain when he comes in. He wants to see you."

Parrott just stood, his mouth gaped open. Captain wanted to see him! That didn't happen very often. We all wondered what it was for.

Captain was now in the saddle more than any two of his hands. He rode mounts out of the remuda and saved Segal. That might mean anything. He was wound up like an eight-day clock. He wasn't content. There was all sorts of raiding activity and we weren't making any good catches or kills. His spy system was now bringing plenty of reports, but he wasn't doing much with them.

A gang of hide peelers had worked ten days out of a camp way up in the San Diego country and had crossed back with four or five hundred hides. That was money. Some of the stockmen were now fighting back for the first time, but they did nothing but lose.

The Cortinistas had a big edge. They had two hundred miles of river they could dart across, then get lost in the back country till they put together a herd. They had a good spy system and appeared to know where every soldier or Ranger was at any time, day or night. And they had hundreds and hundreds of men. Captain had twenty-nine.

Captain got back to camp with Rock and five hands. Their horses were gaunted and lathered, and Captain was sucking a mesquite bean.

Parrott reported to him, as instructed by Sergeant Armstrong. We all moseyed around close, wondering if we'd find out. Parrott then left Captain and went to the supply wagon, took out his picture-making gear, and put together a trail pack. He was leaving.

I sort of whispered out loud, "Reckon he's hittin' the Sands?" Meaning—was he quitting?

Parrott heard me and walked over to where we were.

"Who in the hell said that?" he bristled. "Who said it?"

I grinned sheepishlike and said, "I didn't mean it. I was just joshing."

He unbent and said, sort of low, "I'm pulling out for the Eagle Pass country. On orders."

Sergeant Armstrong jerked up and said, "Whew!" He shook his head sort of slow. "That there," he said, "is King Fisher country. When we go in there somebody might get hurt."

(We pretty well figured it like it turned out. Parrott went in as a picture-making drifter, a circus hand out of work.)

As the fall days came on we were out on patrols more and more, and in camp less and less. Captain kept scouting that lower country plumb down to the Arroyo Colorado. All the patrols were overhauling little bands here and there, but Captain wanted another Palo Alto. And several got away.

Even with all the good solid horses we had Captain couldn't cover the miles of river he was centering on. But Captain was on the prod and driving hard. Our patrols were always for twenty-four hours, and we traveled light. Like I said, Captain figured any man or horse that couldn't make it twenty-four or thirty-six hours without rations wasn't worth keeping.

This old cutthroat Blas was in and out of camp, reporting to either Captain or Old Rock, and we got the idea he was working across the river, setting up kills for this side. Leastwise, it turned out that lots of times after Blas was in camp we would be nested and waiting when a party came across. All that I was in on were small dabs of four or five. When they set foot on Texas they had one chance to quit cold and quit quick. All of them fumbled that chance.

This Pete Marsele that Captain ordered off the list was plenty different. Captain must have figured his work good.

Leastwise he was seeing that Pete got plenty of money. He carried a flunky with him and traveled like a presiding elder. When he was in camp he'd order us hands around, either by clapping his hands or by whistling through his teeth—and I never did like to be whistled at. We handled our dogs that way back in Georgia. None of us Rangers thought too well of Pete.

Time had moved well up into September, and Pete appeared to have something on his mind. Captain was out on a scout, and Pete paid no notice to anybody until Captain finally came back.

Pete went into Captain's tent and stayed for quite a spell. Then we got orders to ready up. Dad Smith rationed us only a cup of frijoles with hardtack and coffee for supper. No patrols were sent out, and those that came in were held. But nothing happened that night—or the next day, which was Sunday.

Lieutenant Robinson hung close around Captain all night, but we couldn't worm anything out of him. "Only the Good Lord, the Captain and the spies know what's on the fire," he told us. "He doesn't tell me any more than he tells you. But there's something."

Old Rock was over talking to Captain when Pete and Blas rode in late and joined them. While they were still talking Lieutenant Wright told us to catch up our mounts and to saddle and draw a heavy supply of shells.

The order came to move out. We left in single column, Rock piloting and Captain next on Segal, which meant something. Rock led out east like he was really going somewhere, and in a lively canter too. I rode many a scout behind him, and he always covered ground easy and fast. He could get as many easy miles out of a horse as any Mexican vaquero.

We made El Rucio along about midnight and halted a

spell for water and a breather. He carried us across the Arroyo Colorado and moved north, now more slow and cautious, behind scouts fanned out in a skirmish line. He cut us back across the Taylor trail up through the Santa Margarita, near the Laguna Madre, then angled us back through the Yturri country right after daybreak.

We had cut no trails. Whatever Captain had come after was still up the coast. We were in front of them, if his spy reports were good.

Out in the edge of the Big Sands was a big mott surrounded by nothing but open country clean to the coast line. The big thicket must have been at least a quarter-mile square. Captain pulled us in there to nest us down. Then he waved us up around him and explained his plans—something he'd never done before except just before a big scrap.

"Boys," he said, "a good many small bands of outlaws have crossed below Brownsville in the last week or so and are putting together a herd above here. They should be along anytime. This is good open country, and we ought to get every one of them."

Some of the men said Old Rock called this mott Amargosa Don Juan, on account of there was lots of a bitter herb growing here that was used for spring tonic. The mott also had good cover, which was what we were now mostly in need of. It was well brushed, mainly with mesquite.

As the sun started lowering it began ducking in and out thick cloud banks, and some wet winds begin blowing in from the north, sort of whipping and gusting, with a little more drizzle each time.

Corporal Rudd sniffed the air, sauntered out in the open, and guessed, "There's a norther building up." He rubbed his hands and hunched his shoulders and said, "It could be tougher than a two-bit restaurant steak. We ain't got any garments to turn a wet norther."

Captain and Rock made a wide pasear but cut no signs. When they rode back, both had on old overcoats from their saddle roll. Captain's was an old Confederate gray. And damn if Rock's wasn't an old Yankee blue. We'd heard Rock was from up north. But right now we weren't fighting the Civil War. We weren't fighting anything but this norther.

Some of the boys had extra clothes. Two or three had yellow trail slickers. I had nothing but the duds I brought up from Georgia and a brush jacket I had bought from Mr. Stillman. I had a hankering to buy some underdrawers, but I didn't have any wages left. Boyd had taken my money, the son of a gun.

Sort of shivering I threw it up to him. "I'm out here," I whined, "without any drawers or warm clothes, on account of you and your damn poker game."

"Take it easy, son," he grinned back. "You youngsters have to learn the facts of life the hard way. Never bet all your wages on filling a bobtail straight."

I caught the second detail of guard that night, and was posted on the windy side. When the wet wind lay a little, there'd rush in a blast of cold. First one then the other.

Day broke heavy and gray. No sign of a sun. Not too much wind. It was almost clear in the west but dark blue in the north, and the air was drippy and chilling.

When they pulled us guards in, I hustled around to the south side of the mott, to break off a little of that wind. All the hands were hunkering close to their mounts, except Captain. He was trying to rest, with his head on his saddle, and he had a blanket stretched out under him. His damp coat was pulled tight around him, and one of the boys had spread his saddle blanket over Captain. He was lying on his side and his eyes were closed, but he wasn't asleep, exactly. He looked more like he was just plumb worn out.

First one then another would go by and look down and shake his head. All of us knew Captain wasn't in any shape to take much of this. Less than three months ago he had had to take to his bed in Brownsville. There sure wasn't any bed here to take to.

It had now been two long nights and one long day since I had eaten a bite. None of the others had eaten either, but I was bothering about myself.

I didn't know much about mesquites and mesquite beans. But the others were picking them, feeding some to their horses and sort of nibbling the rest. So I gathered in several and bit into one, and it wasn't bad. More sweet than bitter. Hungry as I was I went right to work.

Sergeant Orrill watched me a minute, then warned, "Don't swallow the bean. Chew and suck it. Don't swallow anything but the juice. The beans will bloat you and throw you into running fits, and we might have to shoot you."

I asked Sergeant, "Reckon when we'll get some food?"

He said simplelike, "When we get back to camp at Las Rucias."

I began thinking. About this time of morning, back home in Georgia, even poor folks like us would be sitting down to a platter of hot biscuits, some good thick sop, grits, maybe an egg, and some thick side meat. Why in the hell had I left Georgia?

"Sarge," I said, "no funning now. How much longer you think we'll be nested here?"

Sergeant looked down a minute and spit; then he looked straight at me and said, "You recollect what Captain brought us here for?"

"To catch some raiders."

"Correct. And if I know Captain, we'll stay holed up here till the rascals come within gun range."

"But supposing they don't come at all?"

"Then the buzzards will have a big feast, and years later some folks will come down scouring for history pieces, and they'll put some bones together and say, danged if this doesn't look like the bones of that long, hungry boy from Georgia."

Old Orrill was like that. He had a neck like a sand crane, and when he talked his Adam's apple seemed to be pumping the talk out and the air in. He was from East Texas or Arkansas and was dried up to begin with.

Nothing happened all day. We changed guards and chomped mesquite beans and took all the cover we could. I had quit getting cold; I was plain numb and wet to the skin.

That norther never did steady down. It would blow in a drizzle for a while, then change to dry, whistling wind. Like that Texas norther the Yankee wrote home about, first it rained, then it snew, then it friz, then it thew, then it rained some more.

Captain took Rock and two of the hands and made a long pasear. They were gone five or six hours. Captain didn't have to go, but he couldn't stay still. They rode eight or ten miles and cut no trails, saw no signs. Captain wasn't one to let anybody wet-nurse him, but when he got back he handed Segal over to one of the boys to unsaddle.

It was another bad night. Nothing but guard duty and miserable weather. And Captain didn't rouse when daylight broke. Even his cough was getting weaker.

Finally, about noon—in places where there still was noon—Old Casoose rode in from the north. Come to think of it, we'd missed the old man since he rode out yesterday morning.

He brought Captain the bad news. He'd ridden plumb up to Santa Gertrudis and learned there'd been a whale of a big raid pulled off, clean up again into Nueces County.

There weren't even any vigilantes to trouble the raiders, as Captain had disbanded them.

Captain was completely whipped, probably for the first time in his life. Pete Marsele had turned a neat trick. He'd had Captain bring the outfit back from the river and stay nested here four days while raiders in droves crossed from Las Cuevas, and, taking their time, made a wide sweep, burned several stores, plundered as they wanted to, and crossed back with what we found out was pretty near eight hundred head of beeves.

Captain motioned us around him and said in a coughing whisper, "I'm through. I've put you boys through this for nothing. Even if my lungs were good I wouldn't be fit to lead. I'm turning command over to Lieutenant Robinson. I'm going home."

I sort of puddled up. It made me think of an old hound dog knowing his end was near and dragging himself back to die under his own doorstep.

Captain's last words to Lieutenant Robinson were, "Put Pete back on the list."

They helped Captain mount, and as he headed Segal into that norther Old Rock galloped up alongside.

Captain shook his head and pointed back. "I don't want you to go," Captain said.

"I don't give a damn what you want," Old Rock replied. "I'm going to see you put to bed."

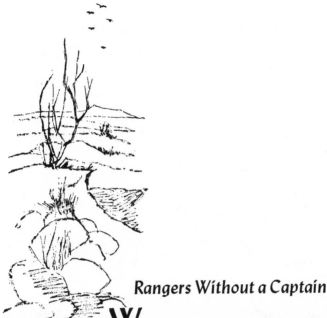

Rangers Without a Captain

We shuffled along toward Las Rucias like a bunch of criminals under guard. Nobody did any talking. Most of us, I reckon, were now figuring on where we'd get a job. Leastwise I was. With Captain McNelly gone I didn't intend to stay on. In fact, most of us thought the outfit would be mustered out.

We knew there'd been plenty of complaints going to Austin on the way Captain did business. The fact he didn't turn in any prisoners was held against him. As I was to find out in later years, the folks who did the loudest yelling for law protection were usually the first to turn on the officers who gave it to them. Folks are that way.

They claimed that Palo Alto was a butcher job, that some

fine, decent citizens were shot down and their bodies were stacked like cordwood on the plaza. Captain could have taken the record and proved the talkers wrong, but he wasn't one to jaw and palaver.

When we finally got back to Las Rucias I'd got over being hungry. My belly had quit growling. I didn't want to be around anybody, and nobody else wanted to be around anybody. We pulled off to ourselves. I unsaddled and turned my horse into the trap, hoping he'd find water and forage of some sort.

Then I shuffled over to the supply wagon and Dad Smith had hot coffee, hardtack, and a pot of frijoles. It didn't even smell like I thought it would smell.

I hadn't smelled grub in—I counted it up on my fingers: five days and nights, 120 hours. That's what it ciphered up to—120 hours. I've known of steers and hogs making it that long, and a heap longer, on mesquites, but this was the first time I'd known of a human being doing it. But we had. I had.

The norther had blown itself out and the weather had cleared to good October kind. We didn't do much talking to each other. Most of us bedded down under the saddle sheds and napped and ate between naps. Each man was doing his own kind of thinking, I reckon.

I finally got a hankering to talk, and I hunted out Old Sarge Orrill, I reckon on account of him being an older man. And I guess I wanted to see that Adam's apple of his bob up and down.

"Sarge," I asked, "what you planning to do?"

"Me?" he asked curiouslike. "Me? Well, son, I'm planning to do what I been doing. Do what I'm ordered to do."

"You mean you're staying on?"

Sarge swallowed a couple of times; then he spit and asked, "Ain't you?"

"With Captain gone—" I began.

"What the hell's that got to do with it? Captain's gone. He ain't dead."

"He's nigher dead than anything else," I argued. "He's gone. He can't get back."

Sarge jabbed me in my ribs as he talked. "You've known Captain about six months? That right? I've known him since before he began growing that beard, since he was a kid your age. He had consumption then—had it when he came to Texas before the war. If he hadn't had it he'd have been a preacher in Virginia. He left preaching school to come to Texas to cure his consumption."

"Consumption," I said, "always kills."

"Maybe," Sarge said. "Maybe. It's always consumption, or a bullet, or something. Most folks die sooner or later. But if you knew Captain like I do you'd know he isn't going to die till he evens up this here Amargosa Don Juan deal and scratches Pete. Captain couldn't die with those things on his mind."

This talk sort of perked me up. I decided not to be in any hurry in getting another job. I'd stay as long as Sarge stayed.

Sarge had known Captain for more than fifteen years, had worked for him as a Texas scout over in Louisiana during the war. Among other things I'd heard my dad say about Captain was that he went through four years of fighting day and night without a sick leave or furlough. I decided I just didn't know Captain.

The word of his leaving at the end of that five-day fizzle went like a prairie fire all along the border. And of course it was well twisted, making it look like Captain was tough when he was winning but a tail-tucker and quitter when he got a licking.

Around camp, the outfit sort of came unglued. Lieuten-

ant Robinson had this job dropped on him and he sure
didn't seem to want it. He stayed to himself in the Captain's
tent. We got no orders and we rode out on no patrols. Old
Rock and Casoose were gone. We felt like Rock would sure
come by and let us know what happened, but he didn't. The
only reports we got now came when a stockman rode in
and reported another raid. One time it was a fight, when
half dozen or so stockmen tied into a raiding party. Two
stockmen got killed, but they figured they had got maybe
three of the raiders. But the party got back across with upward of one hundred beeves.

I reckon Robinson must have beeen waiting for Austin
to order us paid off and disbanded. Leastwise he waited a
week or ten days after Amargosa before he shook himself
out of his trance and said we would begin riding patrols
again.

But our new orders were taken out of the rule books
written in Austin. If we got in the way of anything that
looked like a raiding party we weren't to open fire, like
Captain had us doing. We were to let them know we were
officers and ask them please to surrender and let's not have
any ruckus, or something along that line.

I was riding with a dab of five Rangers under Sergeant
Armstrong when we made our first haul under these new
orders. We were riding in a bunch like ducks on a pond,
back a little from the river, when we saw two riders am-
bling down a sendaro.

Sarge broke out in the open with his carbine unlimbered
and called out loud, "We're Rangers! Keep both hands in
the clear and hold steady."

They gave us no trouble. We fell in behind Sergeant,
fanned out as usual in skirmish formation. We disarmed the
captives; then Armstrong asked, "How many in your
band?"

"Just us two—" one said. But Sergeant let some McNelly in him crop out. He rammed the muzzle of his Sharps in the bandit's belly, and mighty near lifted him out of his saddle. "How many?" he demanded.

The bandit said, "Sixteen all told."

Sergeant separated them, motioning us to hold one, and he told the other, "Go back to your party and bring four of them in to surrender. Do as I tell you, or this man here dies. Bring in four and tell them not to try for a break, or all prisoners die."

It worked. In less than an hour we had us sixteen prisoners. They were friendly, like we were playing games. Which, after all, was about what it was.

Back in camp, Sergeant reported to Lieutenant Robinson, "You said fetch in prisoners. Here they are. Sixteen of them."

Robinson didn't know any more what to do with prisoners than Armstrong did. Captain hadn't taught us that.

Finally Robinson said, "Reckon what we'd best do with them?"

Sergeant Armstrong said, sarcasticlike, "Let's get a law book and read the law to them. Maybe they're just poor ignorant cutthroats that don't know it's against Texas law to steal stock. Let's begin a sort of a law school."

Robinson wrote down the names they gave; then he told Armstrong to deliver them to the sheriff at Brownsville, to be jailed and tried in the regular manner.

All of us who wanted to went along, more to kill time than to guard prisoners. They didn't need any guarding. We took their arms on a pack horse. All of them had repeater rifles and most of them had two pistols. No sixteen men armed like that would have given up if they had believed they were in trouble.

They were right. We rode them down to the jail, and

Armstrong handed the list to the sheriff. "Here's sixteen prisoners we brought you to put in jail." He handed the list to the sheriff and said, "Sign this receipt."

Sheriff looked at the prisoners, then at the list.

"What charge you holding them on?"

"Stock thieving."

"What stock? What brands? How many head?"

Sergeant Armstrong said, "Hell, we caught them as they were making for the river."

"Did they resist?"

"Not a bit."

The sheriff shook his head. "You ain't got anything for me to hold these men on. In case these men had any stock in charge, it could have been stock they bought. The brand owners would have to say different. I can't sign this receipt and take custody of these men just on your orders. We run our affairs according to Texas law—not the way that Captian McNelly tried to when he was around. McNelly's ideas ain't law, and besides he ain't around any more. He ran out on you, didn't he?"

Awhile back nobody would have made an insult like that. Awhile back Sergeant Armstrong—but times had changed. Sergeant swallowed hard two or three times. Then he tore up the list of names.

He turned to drag himself away. Sheriff said, "Where are the arms these citizens gave you?" More insults.

Sergeant said bring them in and give them to the sheriff.

As we started drifting away the sheriff called a warning, "Don't any of you fellers get drunk and try to raise hell around here, else I'll jail every damn one of you."

That was the most activity we had all during October. We had no camp rules. Bunches of us would ride the river when we wanted to, hoping we didn't have to take any prisoners. Wondering about Captain. Wishing Old Rock would show up and tell us something. Listening to stock-men tell of raids above us and below us. Wondering when we'd get paid off and be turned loose.

In later years I got my hands on a report the military made to Washington about this time, when Colonel J. S. Potter was sent in to take charge of the military. He reported about five hundred U. S. troops along the lower two hundred miles of the Rio Grande, stationed like this: a company of the 24th Infantry and one troop of the 8th Cavalry at Fort Brown; the same, under Major A. J. Alexander at Ringgold Barracks, Rio Grande City; a detachment of infantry and cavalry under Major Clendenin and Captain Randlett at a camp near Edinburg, and finally:

There is a Company of Texas Rangers, under a Lieut. Robinson, camped back in the brush near Edinburg.

That was right. We were camped in the brush, and that was all.

If I'd known anything about working stock I'm pretty certain I'd have pulled out and looked for a job. But I was a green hand and was afraid I might not get a job. All I knew how to do was work cotton and gun-fight. I had learned from Captain and the older hands lots of the ways to win a gun fight. I knew I was better than average. Any man that could work for Captain had to be better than average.

A few of the older hands like Sergeant Orrill were mostly what was holding the outfit together now. Lots of others wanted to find other jobs. Lots of grown men had come up from Georgia to make a start after the war. Maybe I could run onto one of them with a job waiting. If I didn't— I'd get along. I lifted my pistol and juggled it.

I hunted out Sergeant Orrill and told him what had been running through my mind.

"You might get a job working stock, which is hard work and little pay for a green hand," he said. "On the other hand, you get to drifting with that pistol—a boy like you gets some queer notions when he's cut loose. Had you thought of that?"

"Well, sort of—" I said.

"That's natural for a young feller. But I'd a heap rather not see you strike out on your own yet. Captain McNelly seemed to see what he thought was some good in you. He kind of cottoned to you."

"But he's gone."

"Maybe. I ain't given up. Tell you what, son—wait around till Austin fires us, or till about Christmas. If nothing happens and we don't get word about Captain I'll pull out and we'll team up together. How's that sound?"

I nodded yes. I liked Sarge. Liked to talk to him.

We didn't have to wait till Christmas. We heard from Captain along about the middle of November, when one of Captain Randlett's soldiers came over to camp with a telegram off the military telegraph lines. It was from Captain. It ordered Lieutenant Robinson to move the outfit pronto to Ringgold Barracks at Rio Grande City.

Lieutenant Robinson read the order, went out in the open, threw his hat high in the air, and shot it twice as it came down. He let out a war whoop and told us to catch out a mount and saddle up in five minutes.

Retaliation

What happened in the next few days
has been told so many times in so many ways by several
folks who weren't there that I'd like to get it down straight,
even if it is pretty late—just about sixty years after it happened. (Several of us during the years collected the orders
and reports to and from Austin and Washington, figuring
sometime we'd write it down, but we never got around to
it.)

The night that Captain left Amargosa with Old Rock
they made it to Santa Gertrudis, where the womenfolks got
Captain warm and fed. Then Captain King sent him on to
his home at Burton in a light spring wagon. Captain Mc-
Nelly let his wife, Carrie, look after him for about a month,
and she fed him back on his feet.

Then he rigged up a cotton wagon with a good cover and came back, fetching her along but leaving the boy on the farm. He had this wagon rigged up to where she could give him a warm bed and good food. He got in Rio Grande City the same day the military made another miss on a herd being crossed to Las Cuevas.

He put Carrie in camp at Rio Grande City, and he took over. It looked like the Good Lord had set this thing up for him. All the soldiers could do was line up on the Texas bank and watch those rascals pull out on the other bank with their stolen herd.

That was when Captain wired Lieutenant Robinson to rush the outfit up to Ringgold.

Then he sent this telegram to Austin:

> Las Cuevas, Nov. 19, 1875.
> A party of raiders have crossed two hundred fifty cattle at Las Cuevas. They have been firing on Major Clendenin's men. He refuses to cross without further orders. I have ordered my men up and shall cross if I can get any support.

A few hours later he notified Austin:

> I commenced crossing at one o'clock tonight. Have 30 men. Will try and recover cattle. The U. S. Troops have promised to cover my return. Lieut. Robinson arrived making a fifty five mile march in five hours.

Captain took back command of the outfit in the fairly good light of a half moon. We dismounted, took off our saddles, and turned our horses loose. They weren't going anywhere else. They were every one ridden down to a nubbin. They were all prime animals, grain-fed, and in tiptop shape; but they had held a long gallop for several hours, the last hour or so under leather and rowels dug deep. They didn't need any holding or herding.

Captain was starched up as neat as any military officer. His britches were fresh ironed and washed, and so was his brush jacket. His beard was trimmed, and he even had on a little black necktie. He looked every inch the boss. He'd maybe put on some flesh. Maybe not. Sergeant Orrill was right. Consumption might flatten him for a spell, but he'd spring back up.

We were lined up along a wagon trail when Captain spoke to us in a voice about as strong as usual. "Men," he said, "these Las Cuevas bandits crossed a herd of 250 beeves yesterday. I'm going to bring those beeves back to Texas."

He began pacing, sort of thoughtylike, and continued, "Pete's holed up across there. I'm going to kill him.

"I can't order a single one of you men to go with me. You were hired to fight in Texas, not Mexico. I can't order you, but I sure need you. I need every one who'll cross with me, every one who'll volunteer.

"We'll be on our own. I can't guarantee to bring you back. All I can guarantee is to lead you up to a dang good scrap. I won't send you—I'll lead you. If you don't volunteer it won't be held against you or show on your record. It's squarely up to you. Take all the time you need to make up your mind. If any decide to go, step across this trail to this side."

As well as I recollect, Deaf Rector was the first one to step across, then Charley Nichols, then Sergeant Armstrong, and Orrill, and Lieutenant Wright. Then the balance of us. Besides Captain there were twenty-nine of us.

Lieutenant Robinson had loaded us with shells before we pulled away from our supply wagon at Las Rucias. I was loaded with twenty Sharps and upwards of a hundred pistol shells. I had my belt full and shells in every pocket.

Captain led the way down to the edge of the water and said, "We'll punt across in that rowboat on the other bank, if someone will fetch it over."

Matt Fleming said, "I'll fetch it," and began unshucking. He went across and soon was back with a little two-passenger rowboat. We began moving over to the other side of the river. It was slow and gave us time to do some figuring, which didn't help much. From all we'd heard, Las Cuevas was the biggest bandit camp on the river, next to the Cortinistas' main camp at Matamoros, and could rally four or five hundred bandits at most any time. It wouldn't cipher up anything but crazy to go against them with less than a military force of several hundred.

While Matt was putting us across, Captain stayed on the Texas side, palavering with the military men. They had their telegraph lines buzzing, with a Lieutenant Guy Carleton working the keys. While waiting for daylight, Captain kept trying to line up backing for his Rangers; and the higher-ups kept saying no, on account of that would be an armed invasion of Mexico and an act of war.

Colonel Potter in Brownsville wired a report that Washington had told the American consul in Matamoros, Tom Wilson, to demand in writing the return of this herd of cattle that McNelly was so het up about. The Colonel said the demand had been wired from Matamoros to our agent, Lucien Avery, at Camargo, so he could hand it direct to Juan Flores Salinas, owner of Las Cuevas ranch and alcalde of Camargo.

"If you'll wait till the higher-ups hear from this letter," Captain Randlett told McNelly, "they might let us support you, if you still have to invade."

Captain McNelly shook his head and asked, "You really think so, Randlett?"

Captain Randlett honestly said, "No. But I've told you

what I was ordered to tell you. I'm just the Colonel's emissary, and the Colonel is the emissary for General Ord at
San Antonio, and the General is getting orders direct from
Washington. I've got to make my report, Captain. When I
do they might order me to use the army to prevent you
from crossing. You're making ready to violate two American laws—one is against mounting an armed invasion in
Texas, the other is against committing suicide. That's
against the law, in case you didn't know it. But we'll try to
bring the bodies back and bury you on this side."

Captain finally was punted across, and with him was Old
Casoose. None of us had seen him since Amargosa, but you
could bet he'd drop in from the sky to get in this scrap.

The ground fog was heavy as Captain moved us out behind him and Casoose. After we had pulled away from the
river bank he fanned us out in skirmish line, whispering the
command, "Stay in sight of the line. Move quietly, five
paces behind me." He led us along a narrow cow trail,
through scrub willows and blackjack and clumps of hardpan sacahuista grass. We moved away from the river, slow
and quietlike.

Some distance in, Captain and Old Casoose came to a
rail fence, and Casoose had some talk with Captain. The
line halted. The fence had been built of late, cutting right
across the trail. Could be a corral fence. Casoose was sort of
upset. He scouted along the fence and found a pole gate
off to the left a few rods.

The fog was still so heavy you couldn't tell the difference
between a man and a tree, except when it moved, then you
knew it was a man. But Captain got a hand signal to Sergeant Armstrong, and Sarge and three other Rangers
moved up a rod or so and scouted out the brush. They drew
no fire and saw nothing, so we all moved up some. A little
more daylight crept in. Our line spread out some. We

moved up another rod or so, and some sheds took shape out front.

Armstrong and his patrol stepped out some more and drew a shot. It was a good loud blast—a rifle shot. It clipped some branches a foot or so from Armstrong. With his size he made a prime target in this foggy light. It must have been Captain who got the sentry—Captain moved in like a cat, firing as his pistol came up.

The camp must have been asleep—with only one sentry out! But I don't reckon they dreamed of an ambush. They were almost a mile back from the river.

They came pouring out from that shed, fumbling their guns. They'd been asleep, all right. There were some horses, but they broke away fast. We kept quiet in the brush, in easy pistol range. Every moving thing was a fair target. Farther down, at the far end of the shed, was a little casita, and several men ran from it for the brush.

Captain held us there. We were doing all right from where we were. Captain held us and held us. He froze us. We hardly breathed. The light was now good enough for us to see there was nothing moving but a woman down at the far end of the little casita. We could see her hand patting tortillas. She didn't look like she'd missed a pat during the shooting.

Our interpreter, McGovern, asked her questions. She didn't miss a pat as she told him this was the Cachuttas, a line camp for the main Las Cuevas which was a little farther on. She pointed to where the trail forked, down a piece to the left.

This put us in one hell of a fix. Casoose had got mixed up and carried us to the right, up to this line camp. There was sure no chance now for a surprise attack on the main Las Cuevas. We had killed several here at the Cachuttas. I heard later it was twelve. Some of them, in fact quite a few, had on Mexican soldier clothes. But that was something for Captain to fuss over, in case they were real Mexican soldiers.

The sun was burning out some of the fog as it crept up, but it was still pretty thick down in the brush. We saw Captain caucusing with Casoose, but he wasn't chewing him out. A mistake had been made, and now Captain had to decide what to do about it. At least we figured it that way. But I reckon Captain didn't. He'd come across to kill bandits and take back some cattle. He wanted to kill Pete mainly but was willing to settle for enough of Pete's playmates, just so they were Cuevian bandits.

None of us was trying to do any other figuring. We were just watching Captain for a sign. His thinking was our thinking. We weren't twenty-nine men; we were twenty-nine McNelly shadows. When he half-crouched and started jogging down alongside that trail to the left we fanned out at arm length and jogged right behind him, our Sharps carried at the ready.

We trotted for quite a piece that way, Captain and Casoose carrying us along right brisk. Finally Casoose halted and raised his hand in warning. He had topped a little ground swell, and off below him in a sort of saucer was the main Cuevas settlement.

It was a fair-sized village, with two sides closed in with a stockade of six-foot poles. There were several clusters of jacales, mostly back on the slopes. It even had a fair-sized chapel in the center.

It had been quite a spell since the fracas back at the Cachuttas, and you'd have thought the big camp would be in the saddle and forted long before we could dog trot the mile or so through the brush. There was only one answer—these rascals had been living easy a mighty long time. Money was easy. Living was easy. Mescal was plentiful.

When we sighted them they were hardly through catching up their mounts and saddling. A column of them rode out from the stockade nearest us. They took their time caucusing and finally sent out four riders to scout through the brush. Not a one of them had set eye on any of us. We were frozen in our tracks and, with some fog still hanging low, we'd have been hard to pick out from the brush by a good fighter.

We all had our targets and had the hammers down on our Sharps. We were only waiting for Captain to open fire.

When he did he got one of the scouts. Amongst us we got the other three almost as one shot. Then we leveled off on the bunched outfit that was still milling close together. It was fairly long shooting but in the range of our Sharps, and our first round tore them to pieces. Every shot seemed to bring down either a horse or rider.

Those still on their feet panicked, the horses skedaddling here and there, the surviving men darting back inside the stockade. Our line was strung out thin and long. We could see good now, and we were about twelve or fifteen paces apart. We sort of dug in. We took the best cover around.

The camp now came alive. They had no leader, no plan. They caught up their horses and rode off in all directions, in little dabs. Finally, a fair-sized bunch got together, fanned out in a fairly good skirmish line, and came galloping toward our slope. I actually don't believe a one of them had ever laid eyes on us up to then. They were no doubt looking for mounted men. They rode right up to us, right in range. Captain got the first one and I don't think they got a dozen shots.

They were coming in blind, I reckon, and when we broke up the attack there wasn't much left. Up to this time we hadn't had a fight—just some shooting practice. I fingered around and found I was running low on Sharps shells. I only had about twenty to begin with, and now I had five or six left. But I had some good targets and hadn't wasted many.

The next thing we saw in their camp looked more like business. A group of mounted men galloped in from the direction of Camargo, behind a man you'd know was a leader. His trappings were all silver-garnished, and his horse was a blooded animal.

Captain rose half up and squinted through his spy glasses. He saw it was the old jefe himself—Juan Salinas, the alcalde. He would put up a scrap that had some sense. In no time Salinas had upward of one hundred mounted men around him and was giving orders and pointing directions. They divided and rode to the right and left. That meant they'd be in behind us and cut us off from the river.

Captain lost no time in breaking cover and leaving in a low running crouch. "Every man," he said, "break for the river, or we'll be cut off. Keep low and don't shoot unless overhauled. Break lines and make it your own way."

There was a heap of brush between us and the river, more than two miles away. Had the Cuevians known what it was they were fighting they'd have cut us off easy. But they probed into that brush slow. They'd tried three front attacks, and that brush in front of them began spewing bullets. That's about all they knew. The brush was haunted.

Back across the river, that Lieutenant Guy Carleton was having himself a hell of a time with the telegraph keys. Later on he wrote several books and stories. He was a writer at heart. What he couldn't hear he made up. He started it off saying Texas had declared war on Mexico, and the sounds of the first big battle could be heard at Ringgold. When the shooting at Cachuttas was over, Carleton put it on the wire that the first armed band was wiped out and firing had quit. Then he said he had a report we were surrounded and arranging terms of surrender.

The American consul at Matamoros, Tom Wilson, wired Lucien Avery, his man at Camargo, this order:

I understand McNelly is surrounded and treating for terms of surrender. Go to him immediately and advise him to surrender to Mexican Federal authorities, and then go with him to this city to see that nothing happens on the way. Instructions have been sent from here to Camargo to allow you to act in this matter. Answer.

As the mounted troops moved around on our flanks Captain had us giving ground ahead of them and not firing a shot. That was a neat fighting trick that probably saved us from being cut to pieces. They figured it was a trap, that Captain was sucking them into an ambush from our supporting lines. Had Captain made a stand nothing could have saved us.

So long as we had plenty of Sharps shells we could easy stand them off, on account of the Sharps outranged their repeater rifles at least one hundred yards. All of us knew now why Captain took Sharps instead of repeaters back there at Corpus Christi. But we were all running low on Sharps shells, and Captain had to do plenty of bluffing for once.

As the mounted men gained ground we were signaled back into a skirmish line by Captain. We were bunched up mostly on our flanks, with a wide gap in our middle. Salinas was handling his men well and began pressing in closer as we got nearer the river.

Captain now had us making a stand, firing one round then falling back. We still had them as good targets, on horseback, while we looked like moving brush, one here and one there.

With my next-to-last Sharps shell I mighty near got old Deaf Rector. I got a good squint on a mounted target, sighting over the top of a brush clump. Just as I dropped the hammer that brush came up and it was old Deafy. He hadn't heard the last command to fall back, and he was still out there in the middle. He told me later that a Sharps sounded like Old Nick blowing his nose as it went by, missing less than a foot.

But they kept coming mighty cagy, expecting the ambush, I reckon. When it didn't come they threw out their advance patrols and began moving faster to flank around behind us. They weren't damn fools. They were being handled well. But this sort of brush fighting was the kind that Captain had made his war record doing. He always kept the enemy guessing as to what he was being led into. It sure worked now.

We were still three or four hundred yards from the river bank when they put on speed to get behind us. Captain told Armstrong to hold two men and cover us as best he could, and told the rest of us to make a headlong break for the river bank and dig in for a pistol fight. At the drop of his hand we all began scrambling through the brush, making all the speed we could. I got into a little cow trail leading to the river and put on a real run, when out in front of me popped old Dutch Reichel, a big clumsy Dutchman who couldn't run worth a damn.

I warned him, "Look out, Dutchman, if you don't want to get run over," and he did better. We made the river bank and jumped down a couple of feet into the water. We were in a shallow cover and the chances for quicksand were ten to one, but we hit solid bottom, thank the Good Lord.

We had a two-foot ledge for cover—but only our pistols, and the odds were building up against us.

Captain never took cover. He walked out front, giving orders, as we got set for what now appeared to be a mighty uneven swapout. We were easy outnumbered five to one, and the enemy was being well managed.

Over on the Texas bank Captain Randlett had brought in about half a company of the 24th Infantry. He did it, he explained later to Washington, only to see that the law wasn't broken and that the fighting didn't spread to Texas. One dab of his soldiers in charge of a Sergeant Leahy had mounted a Gatling gun down below us a piece. When the Cuevians grouped and began closing in on us, Sergeant Leahy swore later, one of their rifle shots landed on the Texas bank and he thought they were attacking his position. He let go with that Gatling gun and seven or eight riflemen commenced firing when the attackers got in close range. The place where he caught them is marked today with a stone tablet:

To citizen
JUAN FLORES SALINAS
who fighting
Died for his country
November 20
1875

Not only jefe Salinas but all his men died there. We broke cover and got all in pistol range that the soldiers hadn't. The group formed for the attack down on our right flank drew back out of soldier range. We heard that about thirty men died with the jefe.

Some of the soldiers now shucked off their uniforms and came across in their underclothes to join us. One I recollect was a Captain Stone; he later got to be a general in the army. The Cuevians were now coming up in more force, and unless Captain McNelly crossed back to Texas it looked like it would be a good scrap. There were lots of soldiers itching to get in it.

By now it was a standoff. Captain still prowled out there in the open. None of us had any Sharps shells left and could only fight at pistol range. But the soldiers had brought across carbines, and they did some good shooting at long range.

Captain moved us up from the water and walked amongst us, telling us to take off our boots and dry our socks. Things had quieted down that much. The sun was shining and a brisk November wind was blowing.

"They've broken off the fight," Captain told us. "I don't look for them to come back except under a flag of truce to gather up their dead."

None of us asked, but some of us thought, if the fight's over why in the hell don't you take us back to Texas? No, we didn't ask. We knew Captain had some good reason. Then we recollected—he told us he was coming over to get back a herd of cattle. We wondered what next.

We didn't have too long to wonder—about an hour or so. Major Alexander had arrived and had taken charge of the military. He was punted across and directed to Captain McNelly. He handed Captain a telegram from Colonel Potter at Fort Brown:

Advise Captain McNelly to return at once to this side of the river. Inform him that you are directed not to support him in any way while he remains on Mexican territory. If McNelly is attacked by Mexican forces on Mexican soil do not render him any assistance. Let me know if McNelly acts on this advice.

Major Alexander waited until Captain had read the order; then he asked, "What is your answer to the Colonel? What shall I tell him?"

"The answer is no," Captain said.

"Anything else?"

"No. Plain no." Captain smiled friendlylike. "Sorry, Major. But the answer is plain no."

"Colonel won't like that," Major warned.

"The answer is still no," Captain said.

As Major started to leave Captain said, "My men began work this morning before breakfast and we ain't had time to stop and cook a good meal all day. They're sort of gaunted, and so am I. If I go back across with you reckon you could let your cook fix me some bread and stew meat?"

Major smiled and said, "My orders are not to support you while you remain in Mexico, but the Colonel didn't say anything about not letting you have some food. I'd chance doing that."

Captain signaled Lieutenant Robinson and told him, "I'm going back across and look after some of these wires and rustle some food for us all. Hold things as they are unless they move in on you. Just hold what we've got. Set up an outpost, and let the boys rest."

He crossed back with the Major.

Nothing happened for some time. Then a party came out into the open under a white flag held high on the barrel of a carbine, and a letter was held under the hammer.

"A truce party," Lieutenant Robinson said. "Leastwise it looks like one. We'll wait and see." He told Sergeant Hall to hustle across the river and notify Captain.

There were three riders in the truce party. When they got within a hundred yards or so, Robinson took Sergeant Armstrong, Boyd, and me out to meet them.

The leader, we saw, was old Doc Headly—at least he was

down in The Book by that name. He was an old filibuster-
ing American, reported by Sergeant Hall to be one of the
real jefes in the border bandit gangs. The doc was swigging
a bottle of mescal and wanted to talk and give advice.

"You're not Captain McNelly," he snorted.

"Let me see that letter," Robinson snorted right back.

Doc took another pull at the mescal bottle—not that he
needed it. Behind his white beard his face was already
flushed, but he was one of the sort that had to suck his
courage out of a bottle, I reckon.

"This letter," he mumbled," is from the chief justice of
the sovereign Mexican state of Tamaulipas. It is addressed
to the commander of the Texas and United States forces
that have made an armed invasion of Mexico. And you, sir,
are not the commander."

Lieutenant Robinson said again, "Hand me that letter."

"How many men you got, sir?"

"Enough to go through to the City of Mexico if we want
to. I want that letter—"

"You have invaded Mexico and killed our beloved alcalde
of Camargo and eighty other citizens."

"It'll be eighty-three damn quick, unless I get that letter,"
Robinson shot back. He signaled us as he lifted his pistol.
We did the same and covered the party.

"Be content," the old doc started, "if—"

Boyd asked Robinson, "If I get the first slug in that wind-
bag can I have those pretty pistols of his—and that hand-
tooled belt?"

Robinson nodded yes.

"If I get the second slug in can I have that saddle?" Armstrong asked.

Robinson nodded yes.

Old Doc wasn't too loaded to know the real thing. His
rifle, with the letter under the hammer, was standing in the

saddle in front of him. He lowered it and handed it to Robinson, butt first.

Captain hustled back from across the river and took charge of the party, still standing out there in the open. Captain opened the letter and ran through it out loud. It was from the chief justice, all right, acting for the dead alcalde, Juan Salinas.

Captain said they wanted all Rangers and soldiers pulled back to Texas, and then they'd talk about the Texas complaints. He had us holster our pistols and handed back the rifle to Doc Headly. After Doc had hoisted his rifle barrel Captain told him, "We'll negotiate when we get that herd of stolen cattle. We'll stay in Mexico until we do."

Doc caucused with his two men some, then he propositioned Captain. "Let's suspend fighting for tonight and tomorrow, that being Sunday. Then we'll deliver the cattle."

Captain now sort of strutted like he was the high general of the United States Army, and he told Doc, "We suspend nothing. The only way to stop fighting is for you to keep your men out of our shooting range. That's final."

Doc explained, kind of sobering up, "Those cattle are penned at Camargo."

"You write out an order for them. Write it and sign it. We'll see then."

Captain himself then wrote the order from a leaf in his book. He handed it to Doc and said, "Sign it."

Doc did. Captain motioned them to be gone, and they went.

They punted across a big pot of slum gullion stew and a dozen or so loaves of bread. We had no knives or forks or spoons or plates. But we sure had an appetite. We were sopping up that stew with chunks of bread when a mes-

senger rushed across, just before sundown, and handed
Captain a telegram:

Major Alexander, commanding:
Secretary of War Belknap orders you to demand McNelly return at once to Texas. Do not support him in any manner. Inform the Secretary if McNelly acts on these orders and returns
to Texas. Signed, Colonel Potter.

Captain was as deep as any of us in that pot of stew. He
licked his fingers, wiped the stew out of his whiskers, read
the telegram and wrote his answer on a leaf from his book
right then:

Near Las Cuevas, Mexico,
Nov. 20 1875.
I shall remain in Mexico with my rangers and cross back at my
discretion. Give my compliments to the Secretary of War and
tell him and his United States soldiers to go to hell.
Signed, Lee H. McNelly, commanding.

We'd just about eaten down to the bottom of that pot of
stew, and I was sopping the sides when another white flag
came into sight down on our left. Captain himself moved
out with two men to scout the situation.

It was a fair-sized party of men with some wagons. They
had come to gather up their dead.

Captain came back and told us to get ready to cross back
to Texas. We moved in the same little two-passenger boat
and was all back just as dark fell.

I'd eaten so damn much I was sort of groggy and water-
logged—and sleepy. It was just about this time yesterday—
just before dark fell—that Lieutenant Robinson had
plunked us in the saddle at Rancho las Rucias. We had
made better than a fifty-mile ride, had wiped out the Cachuttas outpost, and had several hours hard fighting and

running from Las Cuevas. I figured I had earned my dollar and ten cents wages for the day.

But we weren't due to get any sleep yet. Captain Randlett had his boys round up our horses during the day. They were penned, fed, and rested. Captain now ordered us to saddle up and get ready to ride.

"We want to be across from Camargo at daybreak," he said, "to take delivery on the cattle. I don't trust those rascals. They might change their minds."

Sergeant Hall, who knew more about the bandit operations than any of us, seemed sort of gloomy. "They ain't going to deliver the cattle across," he said. "They've taken too much of a beating as it is. They've lost their big jefe and lots of men. They'll be forted for us at Camargo."

We had a few hours to sleep before daylight, since the ride to Camargo didn't take long. I dozed some in the saddle, and when we halted I was piled down on my saddle in no time. But for the first time I couldn't go right to sleep. Things had moved so fast I was sort of dizzy. And the older hands were getting a little fidgety. Captain's luck couldn't hold out much longer.

I didn't rouse till close to sunup. I saw Captain and several of the hands down by the ferry landing and I went down. Captain had sent a note by messenger to Diego Garcia, a Camargo official next in command to the dead alcalde. He asked that the cattle be sent across.

Garcia sent word by a messenger who reported, through our interpreter McGovern, that Garcia had so much business he wouldn't be able to send the cattle across until tomorrow.

"Tell him," Captain instructed, "we want the cattle today, like Headly agreed to yesterday. They were to be delivered this morning. Tell him the commanding officer of the U. S. Army demands them now and might take military action if that truce agreement is violated."

The messenger departed to report to Garcia.

Sergeant Hall was dubious. "Captain's just wasting that jawing," he murmured. "Those rascals' spies have told them about all the telegrams sent to Captain. They know he ain't got any military support."

It wasn't long till the messenger came back and told Captain that Garcia had ordered the cattle delivered across the river at three o'clock today. He was very polite this time. He kowtowed to Captain. He was way yonder too damn polite. Sergeant Hall shook his head slowly. He smelled something cooking.

From down where we were at the ferry landing we could see, back off to the right a few hundred yards, a pole corral full of cattle, and we also saw plenty of armed horsemen riding herd.

"If they don't fetch the cattle across, reckon Captain will try to fetch them by force?" I asked Sergeant Hall.

"Only the Good Lord and the Captain know what he might try," he said. "All this palaver is stalling for time to get forted. Captain is trying to do something that ain't ever been done. We'll see. Yep, we'll see."

Captain did some pacing, fingering the soggy butt of an unlit cigar. When he spoke it was, as usual, something no one expected. He told Sergeant Armstrong to mount us and we'd pull back to Rio Grande City.

What that meant nobody but Captain knew. We cantered back the few miles to Rio Grande City, dismounted like a visiting bunch of cow hands, and threw our reins over the hitching rack. Captain took us into a little cafe and ordered us all a round of coffee and pan dulces, then another round of coffee and pan dulces. Captain paid for it; and

when we finished we sauntered back to see the sights, joshing and jawing like we maybe were waiting for the boat to
take us down to Brownsville, or maybe we were going to
church. Nobody was in any hurry.

But pretty soon a crowd of natives began gathering just
to look. Word got around we were the Rangers. And word
of Las Cuevas was getting around. McGovern and some
others that could speak a little Mex struck up some talk.
They wanted to ask questions. Where were we going and
such. It was just a little peaceable Sunday morning visit.
They knew as much about where we were headed as we
did. Only Captain knew that.

After so long a time Captain mounted us and headed us
back to the Camargo ferry landing. Across on the Mexican
bank we could see two men outside the customs shanty,
and maybe two more inside. Back up to the right a piece a
good many armed riders still held the herd.

Captain dismounted and stepped on the ferry, smiling his
best preacher smile at the old pole man.

"Cut me off ten men from the head of the line," he told
Sergeant Armstrong, like he was buying that many horses.
"Bring them aboard, and have the rest pull back some."

I did some quick counting.

I was number eight from the head of the line.

I had been chosen. It would be nice if I could say now,
fifty years later, that I was glad. But I sure wasn't. I felt
wobblier than I did back there at Palo Alto.

On account of some fellers later writing windy stories
about this Sunday crossing, like they were there, I want to
get the record straight and set down exactly who the ten
were who were taken from the head of the line: Lieutenant
Robinson, Sergeants Hall and Armstrong, Corporal Rudd,
and Rangers Pitts, Callicut, Maben, McGovern, Durham,

and Wofford. I think it was Bob Pitts who dubbed us the Death Squad, and the name has stuck in all the stories.

"If you don't get back, Josh," one of them asked me, "who gets your horse?"

"Who wants him?" I called back, trying to be cheery.

"Not me," Hardy said, "I had him first, and I'd rather walk."

They were still jawing at us when Captain told McGovern to have the old man pole us across.

Captain was pretty well acting like a Sunday School man on a picnic. He chatted some with the ferryman and had McGovern translate.

"Did you go to church today?" Captain asked him. He smiled big, crossed himself, and said proudlike, "*Si, señor.*"

When the ferry pulled up on the Mexican bank Captain jumped over onto land, snubbed the boat for the old man, then dusted off his hands and looked up at the customs officers.

There were five of them—a captain and four hands.

The captain was the same man who'd acted as messenger earlier, except now he had on his bars and customs uniform.

Captain was all polite. He shook the customs man by the hand and had McGovern tell him it was now three o'clock and we had come to take delivery of the cattle, and would he have his boys herd them down and cross them.

This customs captain was also mighty polite. He explained that he had forgot this was Sunday. It was against their religion, he said, to do business on Sunday. In the morning, he promised. Early tomorrow morning they would deliver the herd. He was so sorry. . . .

We were expecting something, but it happened almost before we could lift our pistols. They drew.

Captain McNelly was on top of that customs man like a

cat, his pistol crashing the side of his head and his knee in the man's belly as he went down.

We Rangers had a split-second advantage, I reckon. Our pistols cleared first. We had just automatically taken a skirmish position behind Captain. We were trained that way. Those fellers weren't. They were sort of bunched in each other's way. Bob Pitts shot the first one to clear leather before the man could bring his pistol up to firing level. Bob's shot was good, as were all his shots, and the fellow dropped like a polled shoat. The others dropped their pistols and reached. We shoved them back in the clear.

Captain had only stunned their head man and kicked out his breath. The man rolled over against his dead comrade and jerked back, stumbling to his feet. He was a plumb scared hombre. Captain grabbed him by the collar and hauled him up straight.

Captain ordered McGovern, "Tell this man we're going to cross him over to the Texas bank, and for him to order his hands to deliver the cattle over in an hour or he dies. Tell him also if any rescue is tried he dies. Tell him."

McGovern translated slow, jabbing the man with his finger as he talked. The customs captain nodded his chalky face and head. He savvied, and he sure believed it. He gave orders to his men. They were still bug-eyed and groggy as they pulled away up the slope.

Captain hustled his man onto the ferry and the old boatman was so shaky he had trouble poling us across. But he made it.

The rest of our outfit were as bug-eyed as the Mexicans —or any of us ten who went across. We were just catching up with what had happened; we hadn't known it was coming. It was another one-man show by Captain.

It wasn't long till the cattle were started down to the river. Nobody was trying any monkey business. They were delivering the cattle like they'd been ordered. In less than an hour, I reckon, that herd was back in Texas, shaking the Rio Grande water from their bellies for the second time. Our boys took charge and drifted them back onto the prairie. When we had them well back from the river Captain told Sergeant Hall to take the prisoner back down and deliver him to the ferry.

I had learned another mighty good lesson that stood me in good stead in later years as a peace officer, and that was to get control of the leader when you had a mob or crowd to handle. Never kill the leader if you can help it. Take control of him, and do it in a way so he'll know he's been brought under control. That way one or two peace officers can handle a whole mob without too much killing.

We gathered the cattle and pulled them back to Retama and went into dry camp. Our supply wagon caught up with us the next day, and we began living in high style and loafing around camp again. Captain fetched his wagon over to Retama and his wife took up trying to make him rest and eat good food. Old Rock turned to finding brand owners and sending for them to come in and claim their stock.

As we worked the herd it turned out that they had not brought back 250 head, but more than 400. They'd cleaned their pens.

Mighty near every brand in the Nueces country appeared to be in that herd, all the way from Captain King's Running W to Hale & Parker's Half-moon, from way down toward the mouth of the river. And they were all prime stuff, two-year-olds and better. The raiders had taken to killing and skinning the scrubs and she stuff. These were good beeves.

With nothing much in the way of regular work for us, we began delivering stolen cattle to the owners. One of the final batches had thirty-three head of Running Ws.

When Sergeant Armstrong bunched them I knew he'd pick a detail to deliver them to the Santa Gertrudis, and I made myself mighty handy. I wanted on that detail. But Sergeant was having some fun with me. He wasn't going to take any hinting.

I said I'd sure like to have some more of that Santa Gertrudis coffee, that I recollected how good it tasted when we stopped overnight that time. Then I said I'd like to know what they'd done with that old nag I traded in; that old horse had been in the family a long time, I told Sergeant.

Old Sarge just smiled knowinglike and asked, "You wouldn't want to be seeing that young lady who poured you all that coffee, would you, Josh?"

I said, "No, not in particular. But she does know how to pour good coffee."

"All right," Sergeant said, "I'll detail Corporal Rudd and he can take you and two more of his men." The other men were Ed Pitts and Bill Callicott.

We drew a good trail ration and began drifting the little herd back east toward the Santa Gertrudis.

Captain King and everybody were plumb surprised. That Lieutenant Guy Carleton sure was a writer. In his first story he said it was another Alamo and nobody was left. He must not have ever straightened that out.

Captain King had his vaqueros take over the returned beeves and saw off the left horns, with orders they were to be put out to pasture and never shipped or traded. Those old steers stayed around for many years.

Christmas was getting close, and decorations were going up at the big house and all around. The young ladies were back from school—two of the King daughters and Caroline, this niece of Mrs. King. They wanted us to eat supper in the big dining room, but we backed out. We sure weren't dressed for that.

It had been months and months since we'd slept in a bed or had a chance to wash up ourselves or our clothes except in the Rio Grande. Back out there in the brush we hadn't noticed it too much, but over here amongst civilized people we looked pretty shoddy.

Corporal Rudd was a Englishman with an education. His pants and jacket were of good cloth and they fit to begin with. He could tidy up some, like Captain, and look like a human being. Fellers like Ed Pitts and Bill Callicott and me couldn't have looked too neat with all the clothes in the catalog.

Now I got homesick for Georgia. This was the time when Ma would be doing her cooking for Christmas. There'd be frolics and dances in the settlement. I'd have on clean clothes and dance with the girls.

I'd come to Texas to get me a piece of ground, maybe a few head of stock, build me a house. But what I'd really done was to hire out at thirty-three dollars a month to kill people. That's all I'd done. Kill people. I'd been in Texas about a year, and all I still owned was what I wore from Georgia. Like a land terrapin, all I owned was either on my back or in my belly.

When Corporal Rudd told Captain King we wouldn't eat with the women in the big dining room the Captain had a table in the mess hall tidied up some and we ate together. The women brought us down a cake—a long cake we couldn't have eaten in a month. They'd written this on top of it:

Compliments of the King women

to

The McNelly Rangers

Mrs. King came with the girls. They set the cake down

and looked around. Her niece, Caroline, asked, "Where's that other man?"

Corporal Rudd said, "He stepped outside a minute."

I'd run back to the end of the hall and hidden behind the big stove. I wasn't feeling Christmassy at all.

I hadn't washed up since cold weather had set in, and I didn't have much confidence in my ability to mix well in a crowd. I hadn't been shingled since we pulled away from Brownsville. Sleeping on a saddle blanket is hard on good clothes, like Rudd's; on my cheap farm clothes I had worn up from Georgia—well, they weren't fit to be worn at a Christmas party, or even seen.

I kept hidden until the women left. I saw Caroline, but she sure didn't see me—I hoped.

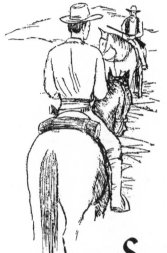

After King Fisher

Something like a month after Las Cuevas Captain got a batch of mail from Ranger headquarters in Austin. Some was from the folks back home wanting to know what had become of the bodies killed at Las Cuevas and if they could be shipped back.

We found out the man we knew as Old Rock was named Rockefeller. His people asked that his body be sent back north. Some of my folks back over in the Carolinas said they'd pay for shipping me back to Georgia. Captain told us to write them and tell them not to pay any notice in the future to wild stories off the telegraph lines.

But the Ranger office chewed Captain up for not making a report on what happened at Las Cuevas. All they'd heard official from him was his wire telling them he was crossing over. Had he let Consul Tom Wilson handle his surrender? What terms did he make? What did he promise? This het up Captain.

He wrote out the report he should have written right after he wound up the affair, and he ended it by asking Adjutant General Steele, "Do you think I'd make a dicker with outlaws? Why would a Texas peace officer ever have to beg peace terms from bandits?"

The fact is that Captain didn't like to write, and that's the main reason, I reckon, why so little is known of him outside this Nueces country. He'd said in so many words that all he wanted was dead bandits. He didn't want prisoners. He didn't want reports. Captain said he was sent in by the governor not to write reports, but to bring law to a lawless country, to prove Texas was bigger than any gang or gangs of bandits. Other Texas Ranger outfits had failed to halt banditry. So had the military. They all made lots of reports, but Captain said reports weren't what bandits needed. He held that a well-placed bullet from a Sharps did more for law enforcement than a hundred reports.

The way the law-abiding stockmen and Mexicans began now to respect Captain was pitiful. They sent down some shiny new badges, and Captain had us pin one on our shirts. Now they knew us in any part of the country we rode through. If they were trying to mind their own business and obey the law we had strict orders to treat them as our bosses. We never kicked their dogs, much less shot one that might be nibbling at our horses heels. We never went into even the humblest house, unless the man himself asked us in.

We had a good camp ground at Retama—like a picnic place. It was well watered and was shaded by a dozen or so big sprawling Spanish oaks. We soon settled into an easy camp life and were living high on the hog. Within a few

miles lived several Mexican and American families, all
hard-working and law-abiding.

When Mrs. McNelly got word around she needed goat
milk to feed the Captain they mighty near flooded the place
with it. Goat milk must have come from plumb over at
Corpus. They'd butcher a yearling every week, and we
were greasing our chin with good steaks and stew every
day. All of us were getting fat and slick.

Right now there just wasn't any more Ranger business.
We rode patrols far and wide without once taking our carbines out of the scabbard. There were still some raiders left,
but they weren't coming across in power any more. Those
that did come across were taken care of by the stockmen.
They had taken on some spunk and knew now they could
fight back.

One party once came across and was peeling hides up in
what is now Duval County, just below San Diego. Eight or
ten stockmen overhauled them and not a one got away.
Other parties of two or three came across but most of them
never got back. Times had changed.

I rode in one patrol of six Rangers that went all the way
down to Rancho las Rucias. We sort of ambled down, scouting the country back several miles from the river. Those
folks were getting a good night's rest now for the first time
in years. They thought Captain McNelly was magic. They'd
heard about him crossing over and fetching back a herd of
cattle. These folks thought he was bigger than the Presi-
dent of the United States. Some of them even believed he'd
won the Battle of San Jacinto.

Just for the heck of it we pitched camp at Rancho las
Rucias for a day and a night. And we had a visitor—Old
Blas. Nothing happened in the lower country that old cutthroat didn't know about. We were still under Captain's
orders not to let harm come to him. He made himself at

home with us. He said another revolution was building up in Mexica, headed by a Porfirio Diaz, a top-notcher who didn't want any trouble that would bring United States troops across the border. He was using his power to quiet border troubles and had taken into his camp old man Cortinas.

It turned out Old Blas knew what he was talking about, because some two months later Porfirio Diaz left his head quarters—in a big house at Brownsville—and crossed the river. The minute he set foot on Mexican soil Cortinas surrendered Matamoros to him. Diaz went all the way to Mexico City to rule the country for mighty near half a century. He took Cortinas with him and pensioned the old fellow for life on a big hacienda below Mexico City.

Blas didn't go along. He stayed on the border. Forty years later when General Pershing crossed over and chased a new bunch of border bandits out Old Blas made it to the Texas bank, came to El Sauz, where I was foreman, and asked for protection under the old orders of Captain McNelly—that we were not to let him be harmed. There wasn't much I could do but give him protection till the Rangers lost his trail and I got him back across the river. Pershing's men killed him a short time later—about forty years past when it was due.

We asked Old Blas about Pete Marsele—if he was maybe in the fight at Las Cuevas. Blas said no, Pete wasn't. Blas said Captain had been paying Pete good wages, and Pete had sold him out at Amargosa. So Blas said he himself had killed Pete. Besides, said Blas, Pete had much gold in his saddlebags and a good saddle.

Back in camp, Captain was pretty well leaving the outfit to the other officers. He didn't give his wife as much trouble as he used to in keeping him out of the weather and eating the good food she cooked for him. You didn't have to get too close to see a sprinkling of gray in his beard and hairline. There wasn't as much spring and bounce in his walk. He sort of hunkered over and walked slow. He wasn't dead by a long sight, but things were slow, and he was taking it easy.

That old cotton wagon was fixed up like a home. Those cotton beds are around twenty feet long, and she had a pallet made with a big feather bed that a man could do some good sleeping in day or night.

Along in January he took Lieutenant Wright and Sergeant Armstrong and drove over to Ringgold. They said he sent a telegram to Washington asking for some soldiers to cross into Mexico and drive out all the bandit nests. He wanted Captain Farnsworth and his troop of the 8th Cavalry and Major Clendenin with two companies of the 24th Infantry. He told Washington he could clean up both sides of the river if they'd give him these troops and permission to cross.

He went back to Ringgold in a couple of weeks and they told him that Washington had busted Sergeant Leahy for turning that Gatling gun across the river and was fixing to file charges on Captain Stone for swimming across.

That het Captain up. He figured the Secretary of War maybe didn't admire being told to go to hell, especially being told that by a pint-sized Captain of the Texas Rangers. Wiring wouldn't do any good. So he decided to catch a boat and go to Washington. And about the middle of February that's what he did. As for Secretary Belknap, Captain said, "He can still go to hell."

Captain was gone about six weeks at his own expense. I never did hear exactly what happened, but I do know Sergeant Leahy got his stripes back and went on duty and served along the border a long time, and I know that Captain Stone got to be a general in the army and served in the Spanish-American War.

The bandit business had fallen off to almost nothing, and we made an easy winter there at our Retama camp. We rode out on wide, long scouts, but ran into nothing much. The stockmen were all busy gathering bunches off the range to put into trail herds, and trailing to the north was now in full swing. They put most of their trail herds together up on the Atascosa, and money from last year's herds was getting back and circulating. Settlements were taking shape and local law was coming into being.

Most of us Rangers had traded and gambled around and had got us some more clothes. I had changes of socks and shirts and britches, but the same old hat and boots.

When Captain got back he looked sort of wilted. He wasn't fired up easy. He hardly ever saddled old Segal, and that horse was as fat and as slick as butter. Captain spent a lot of daytime inside that big wagon.

Early in April a wagon from the Santa Gertrudis drove up. It brought thirty spanking new 44–40 Winchester repeater carbines and several thousand rounds of shells. It was Captain King's thanks, I reckon, for the steers we recovered at Las Cuevas.

Captain McNelly told us to help ourselves and to turn in our Sharps if we'd rather have the repeaters. Most of us did. We did a lot of practice shooting. After using the Sharps, these light repeaters felt like toys.

One day early in April the camp came to life, when Parrott rode in. He reported to Captain; and the picture business must have been good. He dumped two saddlebags out for Captain, but he wouldn't tell us a damn thing—where he had been, what he had done, what the pictures were all about.

But they were something. They were what Captain seemed to have been waiting for. Those photographs and the report Parrott made.

Right off we broke camp at Retama and began moving north behind Parrott, traveling in an easy jog behind the supply wagon. We had no advance patrols or scouts spread out. We were moving through country where you could see two days ahead. Just country. Lots of it. A far piece from nowhere to anywhere. We were a week going through that Zapata stretch. The only advantage was that this was a damn easy way to make a dollar and ten cents plus found every day.

Where was Captain taking us? Of course by this time we all knew. It had been pried out of Parrott. He'd been in that King Fisher country, taking pictures for a sideline and scouting it out. He'd reported all that to Captain. We were leaving the lower country for keeps.

Was Captain dreading it? Did he have another swapout battle left in his skinny frame? No one knew. But we did know he wasn't in any hurry. Palo Alto had been less than a year ago, but it had been a mighty long year for Captain. He never pranced or fidgeted any more, or rolled that old soggy cigar butt. We hands saw little of him, as he rode in the big wagon.

We got to Laredo about the middle of May, 1876—just thirteen months after we had pulled out from Corpus Christi, going into that lower country. At Laredo we lost some of our men, including our scouts and a couple of others who had signed on but who lived in the Brownsville country.

From Corpus to Laredo there had been hands come and go. Some got their names on the McNelly roster who didn't go any further than the Big Sands. Some quit after Palo Alto. Others came on as scouts and spies. According to the list I made there were, all told, forty-five men who drew wages, and I'll name them:

Captain McNelly; Lieutenants Wright and Robinson; Sergeants Orrill, Wright, Armstrong, and Hall; Corporals Williams and Rudd; Privates Adams, Allen, Boyd, Callicutt, Devine, Durham, Evans, Fleming, Griffen, Gorman, Gourley, Hardy, Jennings, Maben, Mackey, McGovern, McNelly, Melvin, Mayers, McKinney, Nichols (Charles and W. W.), Parrott, Queensberry, Rock, Rector, Reichel, Rowe, Saldana, Sandoval, Scott, Siebert, Smith, Talley, Welch, Wofford.

This Jennings was taken on at Laredo as a field clerk to do the writing. Later on he sure wrote. He sold stories on McNelly to a big magazine, and he put it in a book. The boy took it mostly out of his head, and it is pretty awful. For instance, he has Las Cuevas a one-day skirmish, with himself as Captain's right-hand man.

He was from back East and had been having himself quite a time in Texas. He had come down with some money and had bought from one of the boys a herd of javelinas over in Live Oak County. When we found he could write back East for money Boyd taught him the finer points of draw poker, and amongst us we taught him all about snipe-hunting and badger-fighting and all the things a Yankee must learn when he comes to Texas.

We lived in camp outside Laredo three or four days while Captain and his wife lived in the hotel. He had this new hand Jennings write some reports and letters.

Then he came and ordered us to break camp, and we moved out with some new scouts in charge of Gregorio Gonzales, city marshal of Laredo and sheriff of Webb County.

I got a chance to speak to the new pilot and ask him where he was ordered to take us.

"Into the King Fisher country," he said.

Then Parrott told us details of his scout in the Fisher domain. "I joined up with them at Espantoso Lake," he said. "I went from one camp to another and sold them lots of pictures. The main settlement where King lives on the Pendencia is a right nice layout."

Captain naturally knew King Fisher by reputation since back in the days when he helped form the State Police for the Republicans. From what he knew and from his scout reports from Parrott he prepared this report to Austin, now in the files:

You can hardly realize true conditions of this country. It is under a reign of terror from the men who infest this region. This county [Dimmit] is unorganized and attached to Maverick county for judicial purposes. The white citizens are all friends of King Fisher. There is a regularly organized band of desperadoes from Goliad to the headwaters of the Nueces. This band is made up of men who have committed crimes in other states and fled for refuge here, where they go to robbing for a living. They are organized into parties of twenty five to forty men each and form camps in counties, in touch with each other. They pass stolen horses along this line and sell them up north.

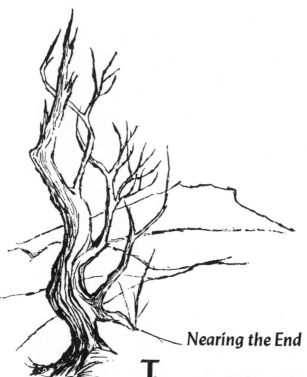

Nearing the End

There was a little settlement near the springs, now known as Carrizo Springs. Pendencia settlement was some ten miles to the northwest, just off the west point of Lake Espantoso. This was an old channel of the Nueces, about half a mile wide and ten miles long at that time, and was named Espantoso (Ghost) because it had lots of alligator gar that ate up bodies of men or animals dumped in it.

The lake was on the main wagon trail between San Antonio and the upper country and Chihuahua and Mexican towns. Many travelers were said to have vanished in the area of the lake.

At Carrizo Springs Captain got plenty of first-hand information from old Levy English, whose general store had been bothered a lot by the bandits. Captain also took in custody a gangling youngster named Drew Taylor, who knew the best and shortest route to King Fisher's layout on the Pendencia. He had worked some for Parrott, not knowing at the time who Parrott was.

Taylor said he heard King was at his house today with a fairly good-sized crew, and Captain decided to round him up now. Leaving only a small guard at the camp, Captain mounted Segal and led about twenty-five of us out for Pendencia.

We rode west out of Carrizo for a few miles, struck Pendencia, crossed it, and came into open country, where our guide turned us north to strike the Pendencia again farther up. When we went into the heavy bush again Captain halted us and told us we were close to the King Fisher settlement.

"There may be women present," Captain warned, "so don't shoot till they open fire. We'll have to give them a chance to surrender."

He opened us up into skirmish formation and moved us slow till he sighted the main house, nested under a cottonwood grove with brush growing right up within a few rods. There was a lean-to running out from the north and a saddle shed and picket line out in front. We saw half a dozen or so men in the shed playing cards. We formed in a half-circle to close in on all sides. Captain raised his hand and touched Segal up a little, and we hit the brush broadside. A rock and rail fence we hadn't seen came up sudden, but our horses cleared it easy; and when we closed in it was almost in a full circle. We came in from all sides.

Most of us had our new Winchesters unlimbered as we dismounted, and I was paired off with Parrott. Darting around one corner of the house, Parrott came flush up with

Frank Porter. He had a rifle, and when he saw Parrott he snarled, "You're that damn picture man." He started lifting his rifle to firing level. So did Parrott. He pulled his hammer down. So did Parrott.

"Drop it," Parrott ordered. "We're McNelly Rangers."

Porter lowered his barrel some, then brought it back to firing level. Parrott did the same. This went on three times; the Porter raised his rifle high and with both hands slammed it into the ground. He surrendered, something he had said he'd never do.

His nerve had failed him. He had a chance to get the first shot. That was Captain's order, of course. He'd have got Parrott—couldn't have missed. But Parrott would have got him. That finished Frank Porter, as he was known. His real name was Burd Obenchain. He was from Kansas and had fought on the border with Quantrell's guerillas and had ranged a lot with the James boys.

A feller he set out to kill up in Jackson County, Missouri, got away, and Frank had followed him to Texas. They said he finally caught up with him here at Espantoso one night as the man was cooking his supper. Frank had slipped out of the brush and said, "Reckon you know who I am?"

"Yeah, Burd," the man whimpered. "I know. What are you aiming to do?"

"You know damn well what I'm going to do," Burd said.

"You going to give me a chance?"

"Nary a chance. Set the food down. I ain't eaten."

The man set his mess plate down and Burd shot him dead, then sat down and ate his supper. Then he just stayed on, and became a top hand at robbing and killing.

Old Doc Hargis, who is still living, I believe [1934], has said many times, and this Jennings has written several times, that one of our Rangers was Frank James, that he and Burd recognized each other that day, and that Frank saved Burd's life. Well, Doc is all wrong. He wasn't with us at this time, and he got his yarn from Jennings, I reckon. Doc was taken on later by Captain to set some bones and keep down some blood poisoning in one or two of our boys. He was with us some in the King Fisher country, but not the day we first rounded up the outfit.

Burd claimed he was a swapout, and Parrott gave him a good chance to prove it. Neither man could have failed to kill the other, and Parrott was under orders, as were the rest of us, to give them the first shot. As for Burd being out-numbered—the reason he later gave for laying down—that was as wrong as all get out. When one of us McNellys matched man-to-man like this is was our fight to win or lose.

Captain saw the whole play. He watched, smiling, as they rubbed rifle muzzles the second time. Most of the other hands also looked on. If it had gone on, we'd probably have been laying bets on the outcome. None of us would have dared to try and help Parrott.

This was sort of new to me, and I asked Parrott later how he could steady himself in a close one like that. He told me what Captain had also told me, and what I've learned through the years, which is to catch the eye of the other feller and hold it. Captain said no gunman could shoot if he was facing the officer and you had his eye. And I have yet to hear of a peace officer being killed by a gunman fac-ing him.

We gathered in nine wanted men in this roundup with-out a shot being fired. Besides King Fisher there were Frank Porter, Warren Allen, Bill Templeton, Al Roberts, Bill Wainwright, Jim Honeycutt, Wes Bruton, and his son, Bill Bruton.

King Fisher quit cold to Captain. When we swarmed over the place we Rangers went for the men in the sheds and

Captain took the main house. He had just stepped in front of the open door when King came into sight from inside. Neither man had his pistol out.

"I'm Ranger Lee McNelly," Captain said. "Lock your hands behind your head and come out." King Fisher did as ordered.

And right there, facing each other at not more than five paces, were by long odds the two best pistol fighters in Texas, before or since. I don't know, and didn't know at that time, whether King was his real name or his title. It could have been either. He was the nearest thing to my idea of a king I had ever seen.

"Turn around," Captain ordered. "Back up. Keep your hands locked."

King did, and Captain lifted out two pistols, the likes of which I had never seen. Gold streaks flashed from the grips; the hammers and barrels shined like glass.

Captain handed them to a Ranger; then he told King, "turn around."

King did, smiling friendly like. He was a prisoner for the first time, but was taking it easy.

Captain wasn't smiling. He seemed fretted. "Why in hell did you give up so easy?" he demanded. (This was likewise the first time that Captain had taken a prisoner, so far as we knew. He was sort of up a tree.)

Before Captain got an answer a woman came to the door —King's wife. Captain apologized. "Excuse my language," he said.

"What are you doing to my husband?" she demanded.

"He's under arrest, ma'm. We're Rangers. Texas Rangers."

"What are you arresting him for? He's done nothing."

King said, "Let me handle this, Sarah," and motioned her inside. Then he said to Captain, with an easy drawl,

"Shucks, Captain, I knew who you were the minute I saw you and you told me to give up. That's why I did. I'm a law-abiding man."

"Shut up," Captain ordered. "You're going to jail."

"On what charges? What have I done?"

Captain was fidgety. He had a prisoner—in fact, a passel of prisoners. It was plain this was something new. He didn't have the answer. There was nothing to do but take them to jail. That would mean a trip to Eagle Pass.

King Fisher's name wasn't even in The Book. He had no record in court. No convictions. No indictments. He was now only a little older than I was. In his early twenties. He had blazed his way into the talk and the history of South Texas in a hurry.

After the war he and his dad had come to Texas from Kentucky. In Fort Worth they had run afoul of the reconstruction police. His dad had died in the gun fight, and so had three of the hated police. The big Kentucky lad got away and began dodging south. He pulled up in Goliad and made his home first one place then another—mainly with the Doc Whites and the Charley Vivians.

The boy did ranch work for his keep and killed Republicans, they said, for revenge.

Sometime after the Whites and Vivians and four other families had moved from Goliad across the Nueces to the Pendencia country the big lad came along, bringing with him Wes Bruton and his boy, Bill.

The Pendencia folks soon lost most of their stock to raiders. They all had families and were trying to get settled in this brand new country. So one day they elected Doc White justice of the peace and told him to try and get some protection. He chose the King Fisher kid as his marshal.

The kid took over. Word got around amongst the raiders and robbers to keep clear of the Pendencia. In fact, where the Pendencia road angled into the main road to Eagle Pass, some miles out west, King put up what was probably the first road sign in that area. It read: THIS IS KING FISHER'S ROAD—Take the other.

At the time we rounded up his outfit King had spread far and wide—over most of the upper Nueces country and clear to San Antonio. Folks claimed he had killed twenty-six men, mostly Republicans and mainly white republicans. He was not a rowdy barroom killer. In fact, he was noted as a tee-totaler. He killed clean with either hand; he was one of the genuine two-pistol fighters.

While Captain was handling King Fisher I had me a little show. I had disarmed and had as my prisoner the one who called himself Bill Templeton, and we'll let it go as Bill Templeton. He was on McNelly's roster under another name.

"I reckon you know me, Josh," he whimpered.

"Sure. You ran out on the outfit in Brownsville."

He said, "Reckon I could speak to the Captain?"

"Hell, anybody can speak to Captain who can talk."

He walked over and said, "Captain, what you going to do with us?"

Captain curled his lip and said, "Make a break for that brush and we'll show you."

He said, "You remember me, Captain?"

Captain curled his lip and snarled, "Certainly. I never forget a damn coward."

Holding prisoners was the one thing Captain wasn't fixed up to do. Now he had nine on his hands. He studied a minute, then told King Fisher, "Call your wife out. I want to speak to her."

She came to the door—a mighty pretty little Irish trick, her black hair fixed in a big wad up high, her clothes neat and ironed. She was Sarah Vivian; she and King had been married a couple of years. (Later, after King was killed, she came to Carrizo Springs and lived there until way up in the twenties, she and her children being some of the best folks and citizens there.)

"Lady," Captain said crisplike, "I'm taking these men to Eagle Pass. They're under arrest. I want to leave this warning for you to pass along—if any rescue is tried they all die."

Her black eyes flashed angrylike. "That's your law," she said. "We've heard you make your own law, but let me tell you—if you kill my husband—"

King said, "That's enough, Sarah. Do as he says. If you happen to see any of my friends get the word to them. Let the Rangers have their own way right now."

Captain told Lieutenant Wright to cut out six Rangers and start for Eagle Pass with the prisoners. "I'll be along tomorrow," he said. We knew he was going to send for his wagon to travel in, and that he didn't feel up to making it horseback.

We traveled slow and made the thirty-odd-mile ride by noon the next day. Captain drove slow all night and arrived an hour or so after we did. We were holding the prisoners down by the jail.

King's lawyer was waiting in the sheriff's office. He must have got on the job on short notice after we brought in the prisoners.

We followed Captain to the door of the sheriff's office. He went inside.

"My name's McNelly," he said. "I'm a Ranger—Texas Ranger. I got nine prisoners I want to deliver."

A man wearing a badge got up from behind a desk. "My name's Vale," he said. "I'm chief deputy of Maverick County. I'm happy to know you, Captain. You are Captain McNelly of the Rangers?"

"That's right."

"All right, Captain. You have some prisoners you want me to hold for you?"

"That's right. Nine of them."

"Very well, Captain. I see you've got Mr. Fisher."

"I've got King Fisher, yes."

"What charge, Captain?"

"He's no stranger to you. He's a damn bandit and killer."

The lawyer spoke up. "That's an opinion, Captain—not a charge under Texas law. You must name his bandit victims and produce them as witnesses. You must produce the bodies of his homicide victims, with proper witnesses."

Captain's fire was burning mighty low. His head sort of dropped like it did at Amargosa. He seemed mighty short of breath. He was whipped.

"Up here," this lawyer said, "we go according to Texas law as it comes down from the courts, not the jungle law some Ranger captain—"

I couldn't help doing it—I let go with just an open-hand slap, but it spun him clean across the room.

Captain shook his head and pointed to the door. "Get out, Josh," he said. "Never do that again." I left, but I heard later what followed.

The lawyer gathered himself up, ran his tongue around his mouth, and spit out some blood. He was mad as a hornet and said to Captain, "These damn killers of yours—"

Captain said, "I'm sorry. It won't happen again unless you keep up that sort of jawing and beg for it. We're peace officers. Rangers. We know the law."

He turned to the deputy and said, "Kansas has felony warrants for two of these prisoners—Frank Porter and Wes Bruton. Missouri's got felony warrants for three—"

"You got the warrants, Captain?"

Captain produced The Book. "Their names are in here," he said, "and this book is a blanket warrant."

"Do you have court decisions backing that, Captain? What have the courts done with men turned over to them under the warrants you claim? Has that book stood up in court?"

Captain said in a low voice, "No."

"If I hold these men under that blanket warrant, Captain, can you guarantee Kansas and other states will send for them in the regular manner and pay for their keep and expenses?"

Captain again said, "No."

Captain turned to Lieutenant Wright and ordered, "Give these men back their guns and release them." He walked outside and just stood there.

King Fisher was the first to walk over, pick up his two gold-inlaid pistols, and drop them in their holsters. Then he shook his belt in place. He didn't speak for some time, but finally he turned to Captain and said, "Much obliged, Captain."

Captain gave him a little talk. "You've won, King," he said. "I'm licked." He studied a minute, then said, "You're a young man, King. You've won every bout with the law up to now. You just might be lucky and win some more, but finally you'll lose one and that one will be for keeps. At least, it will be if you lose to the Rangers. We don't fight draw or dogfalls. When we lose, we lose. When we win, we win. And when we win once, that's enough. The law might lose now and then. We just did. But the law always wins the last round. We'll win. We represent the law."

King said, sort of bragging, "I'm a law-abiding man, Captain, like I told you—"

Captain cut in. "Make damn sure you stay law-abiding, King. You've got a nice wife. You could make a good citizen. You'd also make a nice corpse. All outlaws look good dead."

"But I'm not an outlaw, Captain. Nobody can prove—"

"Meaning I didn't prove it this time, which is correct. But put it this way: anything that walks like a duck, looks like a duck, and runs with ducks is mighty near always a duck. I only aimed to tell you to get out of this outlaw business. The next time the Rangers come after you we just might leave you where we overhaul you—and you could make a better life for yourself. But it's up to you."

Captain ordered Lieutenant Wright to take us hands back to camp on the Carrizo and that he'd come in a day or so.

Wright told us, "Captain ain't doing too well. There's a doc here he wants to see."

Jim Wofford was driving the Captain's wagon. We went by and he told us Captain was coughing up blood now and then. Carrie was pretty much in the dumps. She said old Doc Hargis told her about a doctor up in San Antonio who had a medicine to thicken the blood and maybe stop it from coming up.

Word of what happened at Eagle Pass got back to the Carrizo fast. It built King Fisher up to real hero size. For months they had wondered what would happen if the terrible Captain McNelly moved into the Pendencia. Now they knew. Nothing.

Being a King Fisher man meant lots more to them than being a McNelly meant, the way things stood now. King was on top and way out in front.

Less than a mile from our camp on the Carrizo things began shaping up for a big rodeo and *baile*. They had men repairing the roping pens and clearing the arena. This might have been the regular spring fiesta; then again, it might have been celebrating the victory of King Fisher over the Rangers. Whatever, it was going to be a whing-dinger.

And it wasn't going to include Rangers in the party.

About the only thing they didn't do to us was order us to break camp and move on. But we might as well have done that. We sure didn't have any Ranger work to do—or any that we could do.

Amongst all the folks stirring around the springs now and getting ready for the fiesta were lots of stockmen and stock hands, and all had money—money made in lawful work. Brand owners were busy gathering steers to throw in trail herds, now moving out nearly every day for the Kansas market.

There weren't any fine lines around here to where you could herd the goats on one side and the sheep on the other. Who was breaking the law and who wasn't depended a right smart on whose law you had in mind. Captain Mc-Nelly held for one kind of law, King Fisher for another. Captain had been hired by Austin, King Fisher by the folks on Pendencia. Captain's law was written down in the books; King Fisher's law was by agreement.

When we came in there in the late spring of 1876 they'd had a good winter season, and the country was something you'd have to have seen to believe. It's since been named the Winter Garden district by the chamber of commerce; but in 1876 it was a poor man's heaven.

The Carrizo settlement was different from all other frontier settlements I knew about, in that there were no saloons. That was a King Fisher law—no saloons, no drinking. And we heard he was lots harder on a bootlegger than he was on a stagecoach robber or a stock rustler. Captain McNelly's law said the opposite. Saloons were allowed; stock rustling was punishable by death.

As the folks began gathering for the fiesta on the third day after we got back to camp. King Fisher came down from the Pendencia—every inch a king, something to blink your eyes at. He rode a deep-chested dapple gray gelding that would heft around twelve hundred pounds, a lively prancing piece of horseflesh that had plenty of Kentucky breeding in him. His only blemish was a burned brand, that had ended up as a 7-D.

The saddle was everything a master workman could contrive out of plenty of flank leather and about ten pounds of beat silver. His hat was a brown beaver—the kind built for a cattle king or bandit king. It was one King was wearing when he was killed. His widow kept it till she died, and probably it's still in the family.

But even this and his two pistols, his hand-tooled belt, his silk shirt were topped by his leggings. They were made from the pelt of a genuine Bengal tiger and given him by his compadre, Ben Thompson. The story was that Ben took a liking to the skin while visiting a circus in North Texas. He tried to buy the tiger and the man wouldn't sell. So Ben shot the tiger dead in his cage, bought the skin, and had a pair of leggings made for his friend.

The fiesta was getting under way with the rodeo events when Captain got back from Eagle Pass. He never left his wagon, but stopped overnight. The next morning he turned the command over to Lieutenant Robinson and told him to move us to Oakville. He went on to San Antonio. Eight days after we came to Carrizo we pulled out whipped. King Fisher was still king, and the days of Captain McNelly seemed about over.

Change of Command

After that time at Santa Gertrudis when I had to duck away from the women on account of my clothes I made up my mind I'd save my money and buy me some new duds the first time we got to a store.

Not only did I save my wages—I won back most of what Boyd had taken off me. But I took a long chance doing it. Boyd used kernels of corn most of the time in games he dealt. They were worth a nickel apiece.

I sat in his game three times running and cashed in for good winning. I had plenty of kernels. But that didn't go on long. When I hunkered down for another game Boyd quit dealing, reached around under my jacket, and dragged out a whole ear of corn. He'd caught on.

"Josh," he warned, "that's dangerous, even amongst friends. It'll get you killed."

I sort of whined, "You've taken most of my wages."

"I've taken them fair," he said. "If you're going to be a damn cry baby and want them back I'll give them back."

When a feller's caught dead wrong he gets awful mad for a spell. And I got mad. But Boyd wasn't the right man to get mad with. He was coming up to his knees, slow. So was I. But again old Sergeant Orrill stepped in. He kicked the blanket aside and said, "Break it up. No more gambling in camp." That's what he'd said down at Brownsville.

When I cooled off I went to Boyd and said, "I wanted to buy some clothes," I handed him back a fistful of double eagles, a nice pile.

He gave them back, saying, "Papa Boyd will buy the lad some duds. Asking for what you want, Josh, is better than cheating."

I hadn't been raised to cheat. I couldn't figure out why I tried to. I was damn glad I'd got caught. And I was gladder that Sergeant Orrill was there. Boyd would have gone all the way. I tried to give him back the money.

"No. Keep it," he said. "I cheated you. It's plain cheating to let a kid like you in a poker game. You'll never be a poker player. You're a cripple to begin with. Buy some duds and stay out of poker games."

There was plenty of business in Oakville, but not Ranger business. Oakville was a wide place in the road about twenty-five miles west of Beeville. In fact, the wide place in the road wasn't any too wide, but it was populated well with saloons and a store or two. It was well named as it was in a big mott of Spanish and Live Oak, and there were maybe a dozen houses, or shanties, stuck off in the brush.

Its population came and went. At least some of them

went. Quite a few others never made it any further. Plenty
of bad whiskey always seems to make plenty of bad tempers. But it was not then and is not now the business of
Rangers to referee or stop private, man-to-man squabbles
and fights. If there's a local law that's their business; if there
is no local law they fight it out.

Lieutenant Robinson put us in camp half a mile or so outside Oakville with no orders—and nothing to do.

A feller named John Wilson was batching up the river a
mile or so, and we got friendly. He asked us to stop in and
have a swig of coffee when riding by his camp, and we
sometimes did.

One day I went with him to catch a mess of fish for dinner. He had the fishing gear and also a big bottle of potent
tequila.

I was doing the fishing and John was doing the drinking,
and we had lots of fish and not much tequila left. John had
fetched a skillet and corn meal and was cooking the fish,·
when who should ride up and catch us but George West
himself, the old man who owned this land and about half of
Live Oak County. He didn't allow any fishing in his water
or any hunting on his land. His signs were up. He was raring and faunching. Seems that he had run John off before.

"Can't you read the signs?" he asked John. Then he
turned on me and saw my Ranger badge and really begin
chewing me out. "You draw pay from the state to enforce
the law," he growled, "and here you are breaking the law.
What sort—"

John, armed and pretty drunk, took the reins of Mr.
West's horse. "Misher Wesh," he said thicklike, "thish yere
Ranger ketched me flat-footed breaking yore law about
fishin. He was kinda nuff to let me cook up what I'd ketched
afore haulin me offta jail. I'm right sorrowful, and I'm

gonna give you part of 'em back. I'm gonna let you git down an' eat part of 'em I got cooked."

Old man West colored and said, "I don't eat fish. Turn loose my horses's reins." Then the old rancher turned to me and bellowed, "Order this drunk to loose my horse."

I sort of grinned. "He doesn't pay any attention to what I say. Anyway, he's offered to give you back part of your fish. Sounds fair to me."

The old man purpled and reached down to snatch his reins. John fired one shot, off to one side. "Shucks," he mumbled, "I mished. I never mish a hat at this dishtance. Git down, Misher Wesh, and help eat this batchuv fish or I'll have another try at that hat—"

George West did. He ate a good bit of fish. His fish.

I'd been away from camp all day. When I got in, Corporal Rudd was sort of put out. "Where in the hell have you been?" the little Englishman wanted to know. He was madder than I'd ever seen him. "Robinson got a letter to-day. Captain wants me to fetch you and two others to Santone, for duty up there. We ought to have been on our way. Don't unsaddle. We're moving right out."

We angled over through the Buck Pettus country and rode all night. Besides Rudd and me there were Adams and Maben. We hit the Corpus road in Wilson County by daylight and made San Antonio about noon. We hadn't lost any time.

We stabled our horses with Staacke and walked over to the Menger Hotel. "You boys wait outside," Rudd said. "Captain's in bed here. I'll report to him."

He was gone quite a spell. When he came back he said, "Captain's not stirring around much. He's pretty puny. What he wants first off is for us all to get some new clothes. Don't go around town in these work clothes. He said he'd sure be pleased if all of us would get clothes with coats—and wear them. And get barbershop haircuts. And have our boots shined. He said he'd be mighty pleased if we'd all do that."

This was the order I'd been living to hear. I'd never had a plumb new outfit of clothes that started out mine. One of the things I'd come to Texas for in the first place was to get me some new duds along with a piece of ground—and some stock, and a wife. Fellers that age think of such things. In Georgia I hadn't been able to find any hand-me-down suits that fit. I'd grown up like a beanstalk, a head taller than the average.

Now I had a good wad of money, and I had an idea of some day going back by the Santa Gertrudis. I didn't want to have to duck out when the womenfolks came around, especially that Caroline. So I went to a tailor by the name of Pancoast and had him measure me for a set of clothes—britches and coat. I went to Lucchese and had him measure me for a pair of boots; and I went to Halffs and got a hat.

In a few days I had it all together, and had a barbershop shingle. When I pranced out of the wagon yard where we were bedded down you couldn't tell me from a barbwire drummer. I even had a new pistol belt and a necktie, and I hooked my Ranger badge under my coat where it didn't show.

When I reported to Corporal Rudd at the Menger Hotel, as we did every morning, I went inside and sat down with all the other dudes. I saw Corporal come up outside and wait. He had on a coat and was slicked up from head to foot. I let him wait some; then I went outside, and he didn't notice me.

I slapped him on the back and said, "Mister, you

wouldn't want to buy a carload of barbwire, would you?"

He looked up and his eyes bugged out. "Josh, is that you?"

He walked clean around me, eyeing me, nodding his head slowlike. "Dadburn!" he said. "You sure don't look like a working man." Then he said, "How'd you like to go up and see Captain? He'll be mighty tickled."

I followed him upstairs and down to the far end of the hall. He tapped on a door and the Captain's wife opened it a little. "He's not awake yet," she whispered.

"Yes, I am," Captain said. "Who is it? Let him in."

I took off my hat and followed Rudd in. The sun was up by an hour or so, and the light was good in the room, but I had to walk close to see Captain. He was just the same color as the bed sheets, it looked like.

But he roused up and looked me over, and asked, smiling, "Is that Josh? Look at him, Carrie. By doggies, looks like he's planning to get married! You're a good boy, Josh. You've made a good hand."

This sort of flustered me, and all I could say was, "Thanks, Captain."

In a minute he said, "Don't spend all your money, son. Save what you got left. You probably won't have a job with the state much longer."

I asked, "On account of something I've done?"

Captain forced a little smile and said, "Yes. You carried out my orders, and I carried out the orders of Governor Coke, and now they claim the Governor had no right to give me those orders. So they'll likely throw the Governor out in this election, and us with him." He went into a coughing spell, and Rudd took my arm and said, "Let's get out."

But I couldn't move. I just looked at Captain, and maybe sort of puddled up. I saw him as he was a year or so ago when he took us into that Palo Alto scrap aboard Segal, twirling his pistol chamber—reading the Scripture to that dying bandit.

As I backed away his wife said, "He'll get back to his feet, and we can move him down to Burton to our farm. He's only thirty-two. He's too young to die yet."

Rudd said he didn't have any orders for us. He didn't know yet why Captain sent for us four to come up to San Antonio. "It might be all this election talk," he guessed. "They're saying that the McNelly outfit was a bunch of brutal killers who never did take a prisoner and wouldn't let an outlaw surrender. I reckon that Captain wanted to dress some of us up and let folks see we were human."

Rudd stayed close around the Menger to be handy if Captain had some errand or orders. He told us we could browse around town, reporting to him at least twice a day. But he told us to be damn sure to steer clear of brawls or fights where we might have to use force.

I soon saw that the Silver Dollar saloon and the Jack Harris Gambling Hall were the two main places where the spenders hung out—the stockmen and others who might be in the money. So I began strolling through them both, trying to act like a visiting dude.

The talk was politics and outlawry—of which there appeared to more now than ever. A bank at Gonzales had been held up. The stagecoach to Austin had been robbed. Stock thieving was thriving. King Fisher was the big man most talked about.

I had never learned to drink, and I had learned not to gamble; so I was getting sort of tired loafing through the streets, as were the other boys, when Corporal Rudd said Captain had ordered us back to Oakville with orders for Lieutenant Robinson to round up that King Fisher bunch again.

The day after we got back to Oakville, Austin sent down Lieutenant Lee Hall, placing him second in command to Captain McNelly. We all knew that meant Captain was on his way out.

As a man Lieutenant Hall was all right. He had been city marshal at Denton and had been sergeant at arms of the Texas Senate. He knew his way around. But most of us Rangers felt that if Captain McNelly was being fired either Sergeant Armstrong or Lieutenant Robinson should be promoted. So we didn't fall over ourselves welcoming Lieutenant Hall.

When we delivered Captain's orders to Robinson he told Sergeant Armstrong to take twenty-five men and make another scout of that King Fisher country. Every report showed that stolen stock, both horses and cattle, was moving through there.

Armstrong went about it in the genuine McNelly fashion. He gave us ten minutes to get ready to ride, taking no trail pack—just plenty of ammunition. We got away about dark and made a forced ride all night. He kept us in dry camp all day; and that second night we struck Carrizo. Armstrong ordered us to take in custody everyone who crossed our path.

By sunup we had five persons. And we persuaded them to talk. Most of them checked out as small fry ranch hands. But one, Noley Key, saw things our way when we heisted him a couple of feet off the ground. He agreed to pilot us that night to a camp around the west bend of Espantoso, where a herd of East Texas horses was being held for delivery on Devil's River in a day or so.

He said that King Fisher had left a couple of days ago with a herd of about 150 steers for delivery in West Texas. Years later Mrs. Albert Maverick wrote in her book that King Fisher stopped over at the Maverick ranch on the headwaters of the Medina and Maverick put him up for the night, thinking King was driving his own stock.

Noley Key said there'd be about six or eight men holding that herd; so Sergeant Armstrong left a detail in camp with the prisoners and sent a detail under Sergeant Wright to scout out the lower end of the lake and he took six of us with him. He took along Devine, Evans, Boyd, Parrott, Jennings, and me.

A quarter mile or so from where Noley Key said the camp would be we dismounted and left Key and the horses with Evans and Devine. Then he led us around a point and there, in a good light of half-moon, we ran flush up on the outlaws' camp. They had a sentry out about fifty yards or so, and off to the north a piece we could see the herd with some riders.

That sentry came up from the shadows and got in a shot that couldn't have missed Sarge more than inches. Sarge was trailing his rifle at the ready and got in a quick shot that didn't miss; and the scrap was on. It was a chilly night and they had a big fire going, which gave us some advantage in light. There were seven of them around the fire, and five of us.

We crouched and charged in with our repeater rifles blazing away, wasting ammunition. But we sprayed the camp good. They were all on their feet taking cover and firing wild and wide. Coming in fast, we sort of rocked them back on their heels, and they never did get their fighting balance. Three were still on their feet, though wounded, when we came into the firelight. Boyd, on the far left, hubbed himself John Martin, who'd emptied his pistol and thrown it away and was backing toward the brush, flashing a knife.

Boyd brought his Winchester up as this big Kansas outlaw charged in, but his rifle had jammed. He flung it down

and barely danced away from the outlaw's first slash; but
Martin still came in crowding Boyd and had him giving
ground as Boyd got his knife loose. Boyd said later he
might have done better with his pistol, but his rifle jam-
ming left him off balance some.

This John Martin was down in The Book as One-Eyed
John, a crony of Burd Obenchain and a tough old Missouri-
border bushwhacker who knew every trick in close knife-
fighting. He must have outweighed Boyd fifty pounds. He
was a giant, and that might have made the difference. The
rest of us had our men down now, and we watched as Boyd
hunkered way low, making three quick plunges with his
Bowie as he came up almost behind Martin. When he sank
that Bowie we could hear bones crunch. Martin's left eye
had been gouged out sometime in the past, and Boyd
seemed to know which side to work on.

Boyd was shorter, lighter, and much faster on his feet
than Martin. Besides, Martin had taken a Winchester bullet high on his right hip that didn't help his footwork any.
Still, he cut Boyd. The fight lasted maybe a couple of minutes; then they went down together in about six inches of
water, Boyd fastened on the big fellow's back. Boyd
squirmed loose and rolled fast away; but Martin didn't
make it up. When the fight ended Martin was finished and
Boyd was wobbly and woozy and bleeding pretty bad, but
nothing had got through to a hollow spot. Armstrong told
Parrott to get Boyd down to Doc Hargis.

One bandit, Jim McAllister, lived about thirty minutes.
Seven bandits were killed, but we could identify only four
of them—Martin, McAllister, Jim Roberts, and George
Mullen.

Noley Key was dead also. Evans and Devine said he'd
made a break when the shooting started.

The horses stampeded and we never got a one.

Sergeant Armstrong sent notice of the fight to Judge Doc White so he could look after the bodies. The roundup at Pendencia hadn't got anything; but the detail working back toward the Catarina had got seven prisoners. We now were holding twenty-two. Armstrong ordered a clean sweep of everything moving in the brush; and all our hands could do was let them surrender.

Armstrong lashed them by twos and put them on bareback horses for the ride to Eagle Pass. King Fisher's lawyer might get them right out of jail, but the thirty-five-mile bareback ride might be something to recollect.

He took along eight of us, including this Philadelphia boy, Jennings, who was, as I said before, more of a writer than a Ranger. The prisoners said they didn't want any lawyer; they'd rather go to jail. They appeared to be mighty glad to get from under Sergeant Armstrong.

We missed this boy Jennings after an hour or so and found he had written a long report of the scrap at Espantoso and sent it be telegraphed to the San Antonio *Express.* We knew this shouldn't have been done and would fret Captain a lot. But it had been done, and it got printed in time to get in the governor's politics.

All of us, including Captain himself, knew he was down to be fired. His kind of law-enforcing wasn't good politics. But when they did fire him they didn't say that was the reason; the adjutant general said it was because he was running up too many expenses with doctors and medicine —about two hundred dollars a month since he took to his bed in San Antonio.

Maybe King Fisher was the head and brains of this stock-rustling bunch. I don't know. All I know is that we never did make a case on him. I want to set the record straight on that.

Lee Hall was a good man. But he wasn't a Captain Mc-

Nelly. I served some under Hall, and I've worked for a good many other Ranger captains through the years. Captain McNelly wasn't the only topnotch man who ever commanded a company of Texas Rangers, but there was never another one like him—and never another one I thought as much of. I've thanked his memory a thousand times because he taught me the things he did when I was in the learning stage. He taught me tricks in gun fighting and law enforcement that have stood me in good stead for more than half a century as a peace officer. And he taught me a respect for the law that kept me on the right side.

When Lee Hall took command he carried King Fisher to jail at Eagle Pass either two or three more times. Arresting him wasn't any chore. He'd give up to a Mexican burro if it had a Ranger badge. All the good I could see come of it was to give some Rangers the chance to tell their young 'uns they'd arrested King Fisher.

King ended up as the chief deputy sheriff of Uvalde County. He moved away from Pendencia a little while after the Espantoso fight—went farther up the Nueces and started the 7D brand in the southern part of Uvalde County. He was doing well ranching, had been made chief deputy, as I said, and was running without opposition for sheriff when he was killed.

He was in San Antonio on official court business when his old compadre, Ben Thompson, was poured off the five o'clock train from Austin, howling drunk and mean. Ben was city marshal of Austin at the time. A year or so before, Ben had killed Jack Harris, the big gambler of San Antonio, and he had come to San Antonio to clean up the gambling house itself, which was still running.

The San Antonio officers, knowing Ben and King were old friends found King and asked him to try and handle Ben and keep him out of trouble.

King piloted his roaring friend along Houston Street, stopping with him two or three times for a drink, although King never drank and didn't this time.

Finally when they came to the two-story gambling house, at what is now the corner of Soledad and Commerce streets, King even tried to hold Ben back, but he broke loose and started up the steps. King had run to his side when the shooting began and they were both dropped. The place was forted.

At the coroner's trial they said Billy Sims, the gambling house manager, had shot them in self-defense. But every officer who was around said different. It was an ambush. A two-hundred-dollar ambush.

In the case of Ben, he'd asked for it. In the case of King, he was only trying to care for an old friend.

But Still a McNelly

Early in October Lieutenant Hall moved the outfit to Cuero, where the old bloody Taylor-Sutton feud was again boiling all over DeWitt and Karnes counties.

This was, I reckon, the bloodiest feud in all Texas history. Most of the folks in those two counties were lined up with one side or the other. There were around 150 murders and other felonies that hadn't been brought to trial and hadn't even had indictments returned. Judge Pleasants hadn't been able to hold district court in more than five years. Finally he sent for Ranger help.

What made Judge Pleasant call for the Rangers was the murder of old Doc Philip Brazell and his twelve-year-old

son one night late in September. The doc was at home, near
Clinton, with his family when six or eight men called him
out right after dark, herded him down to his barnyard and
killed him. His son, George, followed and was also shot
down, probably because he recognized some of the killers.
Doc was due to appear before the grand jury the next day—
the first grand jury that had been got together for several
years. Jurors and witnesses both had a way of running into
trouble. They usually either left or were killed.

Old Doc Brazell had been mighty well liked. He had
come up from Georgia six or eight years before, with his
family. He was a big worker in his church and served on the
school board. He took care of men of all colors and beliefs,
day or night, and was known to keep his mouth shut.

The outfit was pretty well scattered when we got orders
from Austin to move in and report to Judge Pleasants. He
had asked for Captain McNelly. Part of the outfit was
working out of Corpus, part over in McMullen County,
where Jim Lowe had reported trouble with thieves. Hall
got together about twenty hands at Victoria, and we moved
into Clinton, the county seat, and made camp just outside
Cuero.

The fact that a whole passel of McNelly Rangers had
been moved in sort of shook the folks up. The name was
enough. None of them knew yet that Captain had been
fired. It put some backbone in the good folks. They demanded to see the murderers of Doc Brazell brought in.

Judge Pleasants was given a Ranger escort day and
night. One or two of us even slept at his home. When he
came down the street it looked like a parade. We naturally
had orders to kill at the flick of a hostile eyebrow.

The Judge ordered Hall to round up the grand jury again
and hold them in session, even if they bucked it. And that's
what Hall did. He had us locate them one by one, bring

them in under custody and keep them under escort. Later on the lawyers said this was against the law, but right now it was the law.

Members of the grand jury got some backbone, and in about a week voted seven indictments charging some mighty prominent people with the murder of Doc Brazell. Named were Bill Meader, marshal of Cuero; Joe Sitterlee, deputy sheriff of DeWitt County; Bill Cox, Jake Ryan, Dave Augustine, Frank Heister, and Charley Heissig.

The Judge gave the papers to Lieutenant Hall for the Rangers to serve, and Hall hit on a pretty clever scheme to make the arrests at one time. It was now only a few days to Christmas, and Sitterlee was to be married on December 24 at the home of his bride's parents, just outside Cuero.

They planned the wedding party the same night as the yearly Cowboy's Christmas Ball, and it was to be a jim-dandy frolic. Hall figured to catch all seven men he had papers for at this party. Some of our hands were still on guard duty with Judge Pleasants and a few of the grand jurors, but Hall had twelve of us to take along to round up his men.

The place was only a few miles from our camp. Hall started us out right after dark. It was still in the shank of the evening when we came within sight of the lights and could hear the music. Hall dismounted us and moved us in through the brush in a half circle. They had four or five fiddles grinding out a dance, and we could make out plain the words—

Salute your lovely critter—now swing and let her go.
Climb the grapevine round them; now all hands do-si-do.
You mavericks join the roundup, skip the waterfall!
Whirl 'em like you always do, at the Cowboys' Christmas Ball.

The wedding had come off an hour or so before, and the

drinks were being poured fast. Now the newlyweds, Joe and his bride, were given the floor to end the dance. The others ranged themselves in pairs around the wall and then danced in closer, clapping their hands and shuffling their feet. The music switched to *Oh, Suzanna!* as Joe led his pretty bride up and down the floor, her long veil trailing as Joe whirled her and hugged her close for the usual kiss.

Lieutenant Hall stepped inside the door and said in a loud voice, "We're Rangers. Joe Sitterlee, you're under arrest."

Joe turned his bride loose, turned to Hall, and snarled, "You go to hell."

Hall said again, "You're under arrest. Come with me."

Joe repeated, "Go to hell, Ranger. This is my wedding night. I ain't coming. If you got enough men come and get me."

"I've got enough men. I've got papers here for six others: Bill Meader, Bill Cox, Jake Ryan, Dave Augustine, Frank Heister an' Charley Heissig. If you don't want to come peaceably, then clear the women and children from the room. We'll take you."

The women didn't panic. A pistol fight was nothing for them to run from. One of them spoke up. "Mr. Big Texas Ranger, would it be all right if we women stood alongside this wall where we could see?"

Hall said, "Lady, you can do as you feel like. I'm here to take out these seven men."

Bill Meader stepped out and asked, "What kind of papers you got, Ranger?"

Hall said, "I've got papers signed by Judge Pleasants charging you with the murder of Doctor Brazell. All of you."

As I mentioned, the liquor had been pouring fast. Bill Meader let out a big heehaw, slapped his thigh, and said,

"Consarn! They're claiming it took seven men to kill one country doctor. All of us must be bad gunmen. Seven to kill one old doc—"

"And a twelve-year-old boy," Hall said, his lip curling, his face flushing. He was redheaded and freckled, and he looked redder than ever right now. Something was bound to pop. He half-turned and signaled the rest of us to come in.

Only the two lawmen, Meader and Sitterlee, were armed. The others had been dehorned at the door. That was the rule at these shindigs.

A woman stepped between Hall and Meader. "Look here, Mr. Ranger," she said in a thick voice. "Why not let the party go on? There's enough liquor and food for all. Let it go on. These men won't run out on you. They'll go with you in the morning and make bond. They haven't broken the law."

Joe Sitterlee stepped up, grinning and asked, "How about it Ranger?"

Hall studied some.

Sitterlee was anxious. "I'll guarantee every one of them will be here at sunup in the morning," he said.

"I might agree to that," Hall said. "Round them all up and bring them here where I can talk to them."

They were all there. They all came when Sitterlee signaled. Hall called the names again. "Everybody here?" he asked.

"Then I'm placing you all under arrest. I'll furlough all but one till sunup. I'll hold one under guard. He dies if you try to break him loose or break this furlough. Is that understood?"

They nodded yes. "All right," Hall said, "I'll hold you, Sitterlee—"

"Hell," Sitterlee protested, "this is my wedding night. I

don't want a Ranger nurse around me all night. Won't Meader do?"

"He will," Hall said. "But remember—he dies if any attempt is made to break him loose. That's a Ranger law."

The party went full blast all night. Hall didn't take a single drink. None of us hands took more than one or two. We ate, and some Rangers danced. At sunup there was plenty of food left.

Meader said, "All right, Ranger. It's sunup. Christmas Day. How much bond you want us to make? We can make any amount. We got friends."

Hall moved all the prisoners outside and said, "We're taking you over to the Ranger camp."

Sitterlee growled, "Taking us, hell. Let us make bond here. This is Christmas. I just got married."

Hall said again, "You're going over to the Ranger camp. If Judge Pleasants wants to release you on bond, that's his business."

With each one disarmed and under separate guard, we moved them over to our camp. They grumbled and growled and fussed, but Hall appeared to know what he was doing. He took each one of those warrants, wrote across the paper, "Under arrest," and give it to one of the hands to deliver to Judge Pleasants.

The weather had turned pretty brisk, and some of them didn't even have coats. "When can we make bond?" Sitterlee demanded. "I'm an officer. I know about such things. When can we sign bond?"

Hall said, "Being an officer, you must know that an officer doesn't set bond or let the prisoner make bond. That's up to the judge."

The outcome of it was that Judge Pleasants sent word back they were to remain in custody of us Rangers without bond.

That started a ruckus that looked like it would blow the lid off the old Taylor-Sutton feud worse than ever. These prisoners were leading men, and all lined up with the Sutton clan. They wanted bond, and their friends and backers wanted bond for them. We had them herded together like ordinary prisoners. Every day the howl for bond got louder and louder. Armed parties came out to our camp.

Judge Pleasants asked for a bigger Ranger guard and stayed off the streets as much as possible. He turned down every try for bond. But he knew it would have to come to a head in a legal way. He'd have to give them a hearing in open court. And he figured that trying to open court would bring on trouble. Tempers were running high.

Some have said Judge Pleasants was dubious about Hall and us Rangers being able to handle a court hearing. I doubt that. Hall had handled himself all right up to now, and we'd probably win a mob fight. But there'd be much killing.

Lieutenant Hall was a good man; but as I said he wasn't Captain McNelly. Judge realized that. The name McNelly by now would do more with an armed mob in South Texas than a dozen Winchesters. And as I said not too many knew Captain had been fired. Judge knew it, but he didn't give a damn. He wanted Captain at his side when he tried to open court, so he ordered a rig be sent to San Antonio to fetch Captain back as soon as possible.

The Sutton boys had brought in two good lawyers, and they fixed up papers demanding a hearing and bond. Judge Pleasants set the hearing down for January 2—in open court according to law.

Captain arrived the day before, and he and his wife stayed with Judge Pleasants that night. Word spread fast that Captain McNelly was in town. It made every one of us feel a lot better. Maybe he wasn't still Captain according to Austin, but according to us Rangers he still was, so long as he might be in the county where we were. Even Lieutenant Hall appeared mighty glad.

The next morning we herded the prisoners to Clinton and to the second floor of the courthouse. There were seventeen of us Rangers, and Hall spotted us around the walls. The prisoners were down front. They were ironed together and stood in a group before the high bench.

A big crowd of armed folks followed us to court. Not more than half of them could squeeze inside. Some of them and the prisoners joshed back and forth. This wouldn't take long; then they'd all go have a drink, they said.

Captain McNelly stepped from a door in the back and stopped at the end of the Judge's bench. He looked about the same as he'd looked for several months, except he now carried in his right hand his service pistol, with the hammer back.

He stood there till the talk stopped and things got quiet. Then he spoke in a voice that carried fairly well. "This court is now opening for regular business. Any man who lifts a hand to hamper its functions will die."

He waited what seemed an awful long time. He turned his head slow, trying to look every man in the eye. Finally he half-turned and nodded, and Judge Pleasants came in.

Pleasants really looked like a judge. He moved slowly to his chair and sat down as though nothing was happening. He opened a big book and said in a strong voice, "This court is now in session. Any person having business before this court, come forward."

A lawyer stepped up and said, "Your honor, I represent Joe Sitterlee."

Judge thumbed through the papers and opened one. He announced, "Joe Sitterlee, you are charged by indictment with the murder of Doctor Philip Brazell, on or about September 19, 1876. What is your plea—guilty or not guilty?"

The lawyer said, "My client pleads not guilty."

Judge laid the warrant aside and looked at Captain.

Captain slowly raised his pistol above his head. We Rangers followed suit, as always. Each of us raised his pistol high.

Judge reached back, picked up the warrant, and wrote across it. Then he said, "It's the order of this court, Joe Sitterlee, that you be held without bond, pending trial of this case. You are remanded to custody of the Rangers."

This was a ticklish minute. Men cursed the Judge in loud voices and called him many bad names. But nobody lifted a pistol.

In less than an hour all hearings had been held and all prisoners were back in our hands.

Then the Judge told Lieutenant Hall to take the prisoners to Galveston for safekeeping. Hall got them under way, well ironed, by the middle of the afternoon. They were in charge of six Rangers.

And as it turned out, that was about the end of the Taylor-Sutton feud. The prisoners were held about a month in Galveston, then they were transferred to Austin. Later they were taken to the old Bat Cave jail in San Antonio.

They got a San Antonio lawyer who went to the high courts and got the indictments thrown out, because the Rangers had forced the grand jury to come back to work—as the Judge had ordered. But when the prisoners were freed after six years they settled in other places and peace sort of took over Karnes and DeWitt counties, ending what was, by all accounts, the bloodiest feud in Texas history.

In later years I got well acquainted with a man who told me the "straight" of this feud. He was Jack Day, who had been a fourteen-year-old boy when it started as a fight between Buck Taylor and Bill Sutton. A lot of windy stories said it was carried up from the South, and went back before the Civil War.

Actually, he said, it began in 1868 when Buck Taylor drove a herd of horses to East Texas and sold them. He had taken along horses from several stockmen, as they did to make up a herd, but the horses he took along from Bill Sutton had been stolen and they got Buck in trouble.

When he came back he told all who would listen that Bill Sutton was a damn horse thief. Not long after that Bill Sutton killed Buck and his friend, Jack Chisholm.

Then Wes Hardin, kin to the Taylors, came over from his home in Gonzales and killed Bill Sutton, and for good measure he also killed two Negro reconstruction police who tried to arrest him. Wes Hardin was on his pistol-blazing way.

For quite a spell it was a family fight between the Taylors and the Suttons. Then other folks chose up sides, and nobody could stop it. Jack Day had a tally of fifty-eight dead on both sides.

But back to Captain's appearance at the trial in Clinton. He stayed over only one day there and kept pretty much to himself. I got out to Judge's house and saw Captain a minute. There wasn't much to talk about.

He said, "If you ever get down around Burton come out to the farm and see us,"

"Are you going back to your farm, Captain?" I asked.

He nodded. "I aim to try and get some cotton in. I've missed two years."

He didn't make a crop. He didn't have money to hire hands, and he got down for the last time. He died September 4, 1877, at the age of thirty-three.

Our outfit went to pieces. Some stockmen made up some

money for wages, but the new governor, Richard Hubbard, had promised in the campaign to disband us. So the outfit fell apart, sort of, operating in small groups.

I teamed up with George Talley, a new hand Captain had taken on over in the Laredo country. George was from up in The Nations and was half Choctaw.

We weren't under orders. We had our badges and pistols but were foot-loose and fancy free. For myself, I was still a McNelly. He had sworn me in, and he was the one to swear me out. Until he did I was a McNelly, I figured—and have figured it that way for mighty near sixty years now.

We were sort of drifting through the country—drifting south, toward the Santa Gertrudis. I was going to show off my new duds to the womenfolks. To Caroline.

We crossed the Nueces at the Santa Margarita and picked up the trail of a little band of three or four bandits who had robbed the Brownsville stage here at the crossing a week or so back. We picked up reports they worked as maverickers, branding stock at two dollars a head for stockmen. At odd times they plundered and robbed.

I naturally figured a good place to cut their trail would be at Banquette, where all bandits come sooner or later. So Talley and I rode over to Banquette. Old W6 Wright was still gabby and nosey and knew most of what was going on, but he had changed some since we last saw him when Captain took us in just about two years ago. Old W6 now walked with a bad limp, and his left arm dangled. He had taken some bullets. But it was a safe bet someone else had too. Old W6 wasn't a bargain.

"I could have won some bets if Captain had been a gambling man," he complained. "I picked out eight of that crew he had and offered to bet that nary a one of them went through. I know seven of them didn't, because they rode out through here.

"From what we heard back here, I'd say following Mc-Nelly was a hell of a poor way to make a living. That sort of work ain't got any future.

"Tom Noakes over at Nuecestown is the only one who appears to have made any money off you boys. The bandits took eighteen of those expensive Dick Heye saddles, and Tom has already got back twenty-six, the last count I had. But he sure can't sell them. He can't even give them away. No one wants to be caught straddling one."

We decided to wait around a day or so with old W6 to give nature a chance to work and fetch in our men.

Talley got hold of some tequila and, looking around for some devilment, caught up a sorrel gelding and tied a tin can to his tail—something nobody but a drunk or a kid would do. The horse got spooked and hurt himself pretty bad. That wasn't any too good, because the colt belonged to Jess Peters.

The next day Talley and I were playing a hand of pitch when Jess stormed in, madder than a hornet. He came over to our pitch game. "What bastard," he demanded, "tin-canned my horse? What bastard did it? Speak up and get up."

Jess was fingering his pistol and frothing.

We were sitting cross-legged. Talley came to his knees as fast as a rattler uncoiling, his pistol out and blazing. His first shot went in below Jess' rib cage and ranged up to his heart, and Jess dropped in his tracks.

Killing Jess Peters was a hell of a mistake, even if it was one of those fast actions where some man was bound to die quick. The Peters family were big stockmen and among the leaders in Nueces County.

Talley didn't say a word till he'd saddled. Then he headed west and called back, "I'll see you pretty soon."

(Well, he did. Forty years later, almost to the day, he

showed up at El Sauz, where I was by then foreman. He'd been in Mexico working as a guard at some silver mines, he said, and as a ranch hand. What else he'd been doing appeared to interest Pershing and his men, who'd crossed over to clean up the border. Talley asked me to go with him to Corpus Christi and see if we could clean the Peters killing charges off the books. I went with him and we had no trouble clearing it up. I got him a job as roustabout on the ranch, where he worked till he died over at Falfurrias in the early thirties.)

But when George Talley didn't come back the day of the killing, I decided to ride on down to the Santa Gertrudis. I stopped an hour or so away, brushed off my boots, put on my britches and a clean shirt, and rode in like I might be looking the place over figuring on buying it.

One of the wranglers who didn't know any better took the reins of my horse and led him away to look after. Without missing a stroke I started walking brisklike toward the big house, duded up like a sore wrist.

Captain King was in the office in front. He came out and looked me up and down.

"You're one of McNelly's men, aren't you?"

I said, "Yes, sir."

He sort of walked around me, sizing me up like he would a piece of horseflesh.

"Are you alone?"

"Yes, sir."

"What," he asked, "brings you down this way. What are you looking for?"

"A job," I said.

He studied a minute. "That's right. McNelly got fired."

"Yes, sir."

"And you don't want to work for that new man—Hall?"

"I think he's fired, too," I said. "The new governor has cut the whole outfit off."

In a minute Captain King asked, "Did you ever work stock?"

I shook my head no. "The only trade I got is chopping cotton—and this." I tapped my pistol.

Captain said, "We don't have any cotton that needs chopping right now. But I can use you. Is sixty dollars a month all right?"

I grinned wide. "Yes, sir."

"All right," he said, "give the bookkeeper over there your name, your right name. You're hired."

I drove Captain King on a good many of his trips to Corpus, San Antonio, and Brownsville. Between trips I worked out of a cow camp on the Laureles division of the ranch. I got to see Caroline when she was back from school, and I began saving my wages and sparking her right steady.

Later on Captain shifted me to a cow camp on the Santa Gertrudis as straw boss—or caporal—and raised my wages to seventy-five dollars.

I did quite a bit of police work for the ranch and learned the knack of handling stock. Finally, when I had some money saved and was making ninety dollars a month, I asked Caroline to marry me and she said yes.

That was in 1882. Captain King sent me down to the El Sauz division as general foreman and built us this house where we both lived till Caroline died in 1915, and where I hope to live out my life. But when I go, I hope the ranch tears down the old house. Caroline never wanted anybody but us to live in it.

And when I go, I'll go as a McNelly. He swore me into his outfit, and he never swore me out. Not that I'd have wanted to leave anyway, after the first few doubts.

I still remember what that postmaster in Burton said when I mistook Captain McNelly for a puny little preacher, first time I ever saw him. "That's him," he told me. "There ain't but one Captain McNelly. There'll never be another. That's him. You can tell your younguns you saw him. If you want to speak to him better get going."

I hope I overhaul him one more time. When I get Over Yonder, as I said, I want to go back to work for Captain if he's still running an outfit.